ROBE

RULES OF ORDER REVISED

by GENERAL HENRY M. ROBERT

with a new foreword by
Henry M. Robert III

WILLIAM MORROW AND COMPANY, INC.
NEW YORK 1971

Printed in the United States of America.

5 75 74 73

FOREWORD

This book is a complete revision of previous editions of *Robert's Rules of Order*, and represents three years of work by the original author, General Henry M. Robert. It was his fullest development of this standard manual. It may be looked upon as the classic statement of present-day parliamentary procedure. The rules within these pages make up the most widely accepted guide to fair and orderly meetings. They are applicable within the framework of any political belief and within the structure of any club, organization, or meeting that must transact business.

Parliamentary procedure, properly used, provides the means whereby the affairs of an organization or club can be controlled by the general will within the whole membership. The "general will," in this sense, does not always imply even near unanimity or "consensus," but rather the right of the *deliberate* majority to decide. Complementary to this right is the right of the minority—at least a strong minority—to require the majority to be *deliberate*—that is, to act according to its considered judgment after a full and fair "working through" of the issues involved.

Under conditions of harmony, particularly in smaller groups, only certain simple parliamentary rules need normally come directly into play. Such rules must form a part of a more highly developed code of procedure, however—essentially because on many issues any group may divide into subgroups, each seeking to have its own will declared to be the will of the overall group. On numerous procedural points it then becomes important that there be a rule to go by lest, as Thomas Jefferson pointed out in the preface to his *Manual,* the presiding officer or chairman be forced to become an arbiter to the advantage of one side or the other, thereby exerting an undue influence on the outcome.

Our parliamentary procedure, or parliamentary law as it is also called, came originally from the English Parliament; but it underwent a divergent development in each colony and state during the colonial period and the early years of the United States. As increasing numbers of voluntary societies sprang up, this divergence of practice created problems which first led Henry Robert to the study of parliamentary procedure in the 1860's.

The San Francisco that he was ordered to as a Major of Army Engineers in 1867 was a tumultuous place, ripe for civic endeavor. Much of its population had recently come from every part of the country and, as Robert soon found, had brought varying ideas as to what was established procedure for meetings. Confronted with this multiplicity of views, Robert realized that a standard parliamentary procedure was needed. Using the rules of the United States House of Representatives as a base, he set about developing a pocket manual that any organization might adopt, "based in its general principles upon the rules and practice of Congress, and adapted, in its details, to the use of ordinary societies." *Robert's Rules of Order* was the result.

It was 1876 before the original 176-page *Robert's Rules of Order* became a published reality, with the full title of *Pocket Manual of Rules of Order for Deliberative Assemblies.* The work received such rapid and widespread acceptance that it was soon identified with parliamentary law itself. There were two editions of the *Pocket Manual* in its first year of publication, the second being expanded by sixteen pages with changes and additions. In a third edition in 1893 the size of the work was brought to 218 pages.

The years 1912 to 1915 were devoted by General Robert to a complete overhauling of his *Rules of Order*—largely on the basis of hundreds of letters he had received for more than thirty-five years since the original publication, submitting questions of parliamentary procedure that had arisen in organizations. *Robert's Rules of Order Revised,* as this general revision was entitled, was enlarged by 75 per cent from the 1893 edition with less than 25 per cent of its content being taken directly from that edition. The presentation of the material was completely reorganized for improved usefulness, and many topics received greatly expanded treatment. General Robert stated that much more work was put into *Robert's Rules of Order Revised* than into the three previous editions of the *Pocket Manual* combined. Upon the publication of *Robert's Rules of Order Revised* in 1915, it was almost immediately acknowledged as rendering the 1893 edition obsolete, and thus it became the work which has been familiarly known to the past two generations of users as "Robert's Rules of Order." Together with the original *Pocket Manual,* it had by 1970 run to 2,650,000 copies in print.

While neither every organization member nor even every club president will be likely to know all of the rules in this book by heart, a person will be most effective in either capacity if he becomes familiar with as many of them as he can. For parliamentary procedure to make its proper contribution to constructive and democratic meetings, it should be followed from the beginning as a matter of course, and should not be regarded as something to be resorted to only when trouble arises.

At the same time, there should always be a flexibility as to the strictness of application of the rules—dependent on the particular situation and the members' knowledge of parliamentary procedure. Under no circumstances should concern for parliamentary correctness be permited to impose undue artificiality in a business meeting. In this connection, the following words of the original author, Henry M. Robert, are relevant:

> While it is important to every person in a free country to know something of parliamentary law, this knowledge should be used only to help, not to hinder business. One who

> is constantly raising points of order and insisting upon a strict observance of every rule in a peaceable asesmbly in which most of the members are . . . [unfamiliar with] these rules and customs, makes himself a nuisance, hinders business, and prejudices people against parliamentary law. Such a person . . . either . . . [does not understand] its real purpose or else wilfully misuses his knowledge.

The reader will find the elementary rules for the conduct of business stated in the first ten sections of this book, pages 25–51. After studying this material, he should learn the names and purposes of the different parliamentary motions as explained in the succeeding sections and should become familiar with the Order of Precedence of Motions on page 5 and the Table of Rules Relating to Motions, pages 6–12. A series of lesson outlines for the study of parliamentary procedure is given on pages 305–12.

This edition of *Robert's Rules of Order Revised* has been made by direct photographic reproduction from the 1915 edition, keeping the same pagination so that all page references to the 1915 edition apply equally to this book.

A more fully explicated statement of these rules will be found in *Robert's Rules of Order Newly Revised* (1970).

HENRY M. ROBERT III
Chief Advisory Editor,
Robert's Rules of Order Newly Revised

TABLE OF CONTENTS

Part II.—Organization, Meetings, and Legal Rights of Assemblies.

Art. XII.—Organization and Meetings.

Art. XIII.—Legal Rights of Assemblies and Trial of Their Members.

Plan for Study of Parliamentary Law.

ORDER OF PRECEDENCE OF MOTIONS.

The ordinary motions rank as follows, the lowest in rank being at the bottom and the highest at the top of the list. When any one of them is immediately pending the motions above it in the list are in order, and those below are out of order. Those marked (⅔) require a ⅔ vote for their adoption; the others require only a majority.

	Motion	
Undebatable	**Fix the Time to which to Adjourn (when privileged).* †**	Privileged †
	Adjourn (when privileged).†	
	Take a Recess (when privileged).* †	
	Raise a Question of Privilege.	
	Call for the Orders of the Day.	
	Lay on the Table.	Subsidiary
	Previous Question (2/3).	
	Limit or Extend Limits of Debate (2/3).*	
Debatable	**Postpone to a Certain Time.***	
	Commit or Refer.*	
	Amend.*	
	Postpone Indefinitely.	
	A Main Motion.*	

---

* Can be amended: the others cannot be amended.

† The first three motions are not always privileged. To *Fix the Time to which to Adjourn* is privileged only when made while another question is pending, and in an assembly that has made no provision for another meeting on the same or the next day. To *Adjourn* loses its privileged character and is a main motion if in any way qualified, or if its effect, if adopted, is to dissolve the assembly without any provision for its meeting again. To *Take a Recess* is privileged only when made while other business is pending.

TABLE OF RULES RELATING TO MOTIONS

Answering 300 Questions in Parliamentary Practice

Explanation of the Table.—The rules at the head of the 8 columns apply to all original main motions, and to all other cases except where a star (★) or a figure indicates that the motion is an exception to these rules. The star shows that the exact opposite of the rule at the head of the column applies to the motion, and a figure refers to a note which explains the extent of the exception. For example, "Lay on the Table"; the Table shows that § 28 of the Manual treats of this motion; that it is "undebatable" and "cannot be amended"; that "no subsidiary motion can be applied" to it; and that it "cannot be reconsidered";—the fact that the 4 other columns have no stars or figures shows that the rules at the head of these columns apply to this motion, to Lay on the Table, the same as to original main motions.

[See pages 11 and 12 for a fuller explanation.]

Section in Rules of Order, Revised.		Debatable.	Debate Confined to Pending Question.	Can be Amended.	Subsidiary Motions can be Applied.	Can be Reconsidered.	Requires only a Majority Vote.	Must be Seconded.	Out of Order when Another has Floor.
17	Adjourn (when privileged) 1	★	—	★	★	★	—	—	—
54	Adopt (Accept or Agree to) a Report	—	—	—	—	—	—	—	—
67	Adopt Constitutions, By-laws, Rules of Order . .	—	—	—	—	2	—	—	—
67	Adopt Standing Rules	—	—	—	—	—	—	—	—

33	Amend[3]	4	—	—	—	—	—	—	—
33	Amend an Amendment	4	—	★	—	—	—	—	—
68	Amend Constitutions, By-laws, Rules of Order	—	—	—	—	2	5	—	—
67	Amend Standing Rules	—	—	—	—	—	6	—	—
21	Appeal, relating to Indecorum, etc[7]	★	—	★	—	—	—	—	★
21	Appeal, all other cases	—	—	★	—	—	—	—	★
33	Blanks, Filling	—	—	★	—	—	—	★	—
32	Commit or Refer, or Recommit	—	—	—	—	8	—	—	—
30	Debate, to Close, Limit, or Extend[9]	★	—	—	—	—	★	—	—
25	Division of the Assembly	★	—	★	★	★	—	★	★
24	Division of the Question	★	—	—	—	★	—	10	10
16	Fix the Time to which to Adjourn[1]	11	—	—	—	—	—	—	—
57	Informal Consideration of a Question	—	—	★	—	2	—	—	—
28	Lay on the Table	★	—	★	★	★	—	—	—
21	Leave to Continue Speaking after Indecorum	★	—	★	★	—	—	—	—
11	Main Motion or Question	—	—	—	—	—	—	—	—
26	Nominations, to Make	—	—	★	—	★	—	★	—
26	Nominations, to Close	★	—	—	—	★	★	—	—
26	Nominations, to Reopen	★	—	—	—	2	—	—	—
23	Objection to Consideration of a Question	★	—	★	★	2	12	★	★

(Continued.)

21	Order, Questions of	★	—	★	★	★	—	★	★
20	Order, to Make a Special	—	—	—	—	—	★	—	—
20	Orders of the Day, to Call for	★	—	★	★	★	—	★	★
20	Order of the Day, when pending	—	—	—	—	—	—	—	—
27	Parliamentary Inquiry	★	—	★	★	★	—	★	★
31	Postpone Definitely, or to a Certain Time	—	—	—	—	—	—	—	—
34	Postpone Indefinitely	—	★	★	—	13	—	—	—
29	Previous Question 14	★	—	★	★	15	★	—	—
19	Privilege, to Raise Questions of	★	—	★	★	★	—	★	★
19	Privilege, Questions of, when pending	—	—	—	—	—	—	—	—
27	Reading Papers	★	—	★	★	—	—	—	—
18	Recess, to Take a (when privileged) 1	11	—	—	—	★	—	—	—
36	Reconsider 16	4	17	★	—	★	—	—	★
37	Rescind or Repeal	—	★	—	—	2	18	—	—
33	Substitute (same as Amend)	—	—	—	—	—	—	—	—
22	Suspend the Rules	★	—	★	★	★	★	—	—
35	Take from the Table	★	—	★	★	★	—	—	—
22	Take up a Question out of its Proper Order	★	—	★	★	★	★	—	—
25	Voting, Motions relating to	★	—	—	—	—	—	—	—
27	Withdraw a Motion, Leave to	★	—	★	★	2	—	★	—

NOTES TO TABLE

1 See last footnote on page 5.

2 An affirmative vote on this motion cannot be reconsidered.

3 An Amendment may be made (*a*) by *inserting* (or *adding*) words or paragraphs; (*b*) by *striking out* words or paragraphs; (*c*) by *striking out certain words* and *inserting others;* or (*d*) by *substituting* one or more paragraphs for others, or an entire resolution for another, on the same subject.

4 Undebatable when the motion to be amended or reconsidered is undebatable.

5 Constitutions, By-Laws, and Rules of Order before adoption are in every respect main motions and may be amended by majority vote. After adoption they require previous notice and ⅔ vote for amendment.

6 Standing Rules may be amended at any time by a majority vote if previous notice has been given, or by a ⅔ vote without notice.

7 An Appeal is undebatable only when made while an undebatable question is pending, or when relating to indecorum, or to transgressions of the rules of speaking, or to the priority of business. When debatable, only one speech from each member is permitted. On a tie vote the decision of the chair is sustained.

8 Cannot be reconsidered after the committee has taken up the subject, but by ⅔ vote the committee at any time may be discharged from further consideration of the question.

9 These motions may be moved whenever the immediately pending question is debatable, and they apply only to it, unless otherwise specified.

10 If resolutions or propositions relate to different subjects which are independent of each other, they must be divided on the request of a single member, which can be made when another has the floor. If they relate to the same subject and yet each part can stand alone, they may be divided only on a regular motion and vote.

11 Undebatable if made when another question is before the assembly.

12 The objection can be made only when the question is first introduced, before debate. A ⅔ vote must be opposed to the

consideration in order to sustain the objection.

13 A negative vote on this motion cannot be reconsidered.

14 The Previous Question may be moved whenever the immediately pending question is debatable or amendable. The questions upon which it is moved should be specified; if not specified, it applies only to the immediately pending question. If adopted it cuts off debate and at once brings the assembly to a vote on the immediately pending question and such others as are specified in the motion.

15 Cannot be reconsidered after a vote has been taken under it.

16 The motion to reconsider can be made while any other question is before the assembly, and even while another has the floor, or after it has been voted to adjourn, provided the assembly has not been declared adjourned. It can be moved only on the day, or the day after, the vote which it is proposed to reconsider was taken, and by one who voted with the prevailing side. Its consideration cannot interrupt business unless the motion to be reconsidered takes precedence of the immediately pending question. Its rank is the same as that of the motion to be reconsidered, except that it takes precedence of a general order, or of a motion of equal rank with the motion to be reconsidered, provided their consideration has not actually begun.

17 Opens to debate main question when latter is debatable.

18 Rescind is under the same rules as to amend something already adopted. See notes 2, 5, and 6, above.

ADDITIONAL RULES

Incidental Motions. Motions that are incidental to pending motions take precedence of them and must be acted upon first. [See 13 for list of these motions.]

No privileged or subsidiary motion can be laid on the table, postponed definitely or indefinitely, or committed. When the main question is laid on the table, etc., all adhering subsidiaries go with it.

EXPLANATION OF THE TABLE OF RULES RELATING TO MOTIONS.

Every one expecting to take an active part in meetings of a deliberative assembly should become sufficiently familiar with the Order of Precedence of Motions, page 5, and the Table of Rules, pages 6-10, to be able to refer to them quickly. This familiarity can only be acquired by actual practice in referring to these tables and finding the rulings on the various points covered by them in regard to various motions. These six pages contain an epitome of parliamentary law. The Order of Precedence of Motions should be committed to memory, as it contains all of the privileged and subsidiary motions, 12 in number, arranged in their order of rank, and shows in regard to each motion whether it can be debated or amended, and what vote it requires, and under what circumstances it can be made.

In the Table of Rules the headings to the 8 columns are rules or principles which are applicable to all original main motions, and should be memorized. They are as follows: (1) Original Main Motions are debatable; (2) debate must be confined to the immediately pending question; (3) they can be amended; (4) all subsidiary motions can be applied to them; (5) they can be reconsidered; (6) they require only a majority vote for their adoption; (7) they must be seconded; and (8) they are not in order when another has the floor. Whenever any of the 44 motions in the Table differs from a main motion in regard to any of these rules, the exception is indicated by a star (*) or a figure in the proper column opposite that motion. A star shows that the exact opposite of the rule at the head of the column applies to the motion. A figure refers to a note which explains the extent of the exception. A blank shows that the rule at the head of the column applies, and therefore that the motion is in this respect exactly like a main motion.

Some of the motions are followed by figures not in the columns: these figures refer to notes giving useful information in regard to these motions.

The Table of Rules is constructed upon the theory that it is best to learn the general principles of parliamentary law as applied to original main motions, and then to note in what respects each other motion is an exception to these general rules. Thus, the motion to postpone definitely, or to a certain time, has no stars or figures opposite it, and therefore it is subject to all of the above 8 rules the same as any main motion: to postpone indefinitely has two stars and the number 13 opposite to it, showing that the rules at the head of these three columns do not apply to this motion. The first star shows that debate is not confined to the motion to postpone indefinitely, but that the main motion is also open to debate; the second star shows that the motion to postpone indefinitely cannot be amended; and the number 13 refers to a note which shows that a negative vote on this motion cannot be reconsidered.

As has previously been stated, a star shows that the motion, instead of being subject to the rule at the head of the column, is subject to a rule exactly the reverse. Stars in the various columns, therefore, mean that the motions are subject to the following rules: (1) undebatable; (2) opens main question to debate; (3) cannot be amended; (4) no subsidiary motion can be applied; (5) cannot be reconsidered; (6) requires a two-thirds vote; (7) does not require to be seconded; and (8) in order when another has the floor.

PREFACE.

A work on parliamentary law is needed, based, in its general principles, upon the rules and practice of Congress, but adapted, in its details, to the use of ordinary societies. Such a work should give not only the methods of organizing and conducting meetings, the duties of officers, and names of ordinary motions, but also a systematic statement in reference to each motion, as to its object and effect; whether it can be amended or debated; if debatable, the extent to which it opens the main question to debate; the circumstances under which it can be made, and what other motions can be made while it is pending. Robert's Rules of Order (published in 1876, slight additions being made in 1893) was prepared with a hope of supplying the above information in a condensed and systematic form, each rule being complete in itself, or giving references to every section that in any way qualifies it, so that a stranger to the work can refer to any special subject with safety.

The fact that during these thirty-nine years a half million copies of these Rules have been published would indicate that there is a demand for a work of this kind. But the constant inquiries from all sections of the country for information concerning proceedings in deliberative assemblies that is not contained in Rules of Order, seems to demand a revision and enlargement of the manual. To meet this want, the work has been thoroughly revised and enlarged, and, to avoid confusion with the old Rules, is published under the title of "Robert's Rules of Order Revised."

The object of Rules of Order is to assist an assembly to accomplish in the best possible manner the work for which it was designed. To do this it is necessary to restrain the individual somewhat, as the right of an individual, in any community, to do what he pleases, is incompatible with the interests of the whole. Where there is no law, but every man does what is right in his own eyes, there is the least of real liberty. Experience has shown the importance of definiteness in the law; and in this country, where customs are so slightly established and the published manuals of parliamentary practice so conflicting, no society should attempt to conduct business without having adopted some work upon the subject as the authority in all cases not covered by its own special rules.

While it is important that an assembly has good rules, it is more important that it be not without some rules to govern its proceedings. It is much more important, for instance, that an assembly has a rule determining the rank of the motion to postpone indefinitely, than that it gives this motion the highest rank of all subsidiary motions except to lay on the table, as in the U. S. Senate; or gives it the lowest rank, as in the U. S. House of Representatives; or gives it equal rank with the previous question, to postpone definitely, and to commit, so that if one is pending none of the others may be moved, as under the old parliamentary law. This has been well expressed by one of the greatest of English writers on parliamentary law: "Whether these forms be in all cases the most rational or not is really not of so great importance. It is much more material that there should be a rule to go by than what that rule is; that there may be a uniformity of proceeding in business, not subject to the caprice of the chairman or captiousness of the members. It is very material that order, decency, and regularity be preserved in a dignified public body."

H. M. R.

February, 1915.

INTRODUCTION.

PARLIAMENTARY LAW.

Parliamentary Law refers originally to the customs and rules for conducting business in the English Parliament; and thence to the usages of deliberative assemblies in general. In England these usages of Parliament form a part of the unwritten law of the land, and in our own legislative bodies they are of authority in all cases where they do not conflict with existing rules or precedents.

But as a people we have not the respect which the English have for customs and precedents, and are always ready for such innovations as we think are improvements; hence changes have been and are constantly being made in the written rules which our legislative bodies have found best to adopt. As each house adopts its own rules, the result is that the two houses of the same legislature do not always agree in their practice; even in Congress the order of precedence of motions is not the same in both houses, and the previous question is admitted in the House of Representatives but not in the Senate. As a consequence of this, the exact method of conducting business in any particular legislative body is to be obtained only from the Legislative Manual of that body.

The vast number of societies—political, literary, scientific, benevolent, and religious—formed all over the land, though not legislative, are deliberative in character, and must have some system of conducting business and some rules to govern their proceedings, and are necessarily subject to the common parliamentary law where it does not conflict with their own special rules. But as their knowledge of parliamentary law has been obtained from the usages in this country, rather than from the customs of Parliament, it has resulted that these societies have followed in part the customs of our own legislative bodies, and our people have thus been educated under a system of parliamentary law which is peculiar to this country, and yet so well established as to supersede the English parliamentary law as the common law of ordinary deliberative assemblies.

The practice of the National House of Representatives should have the same force in this country as the usages of the House of Commons have in England, in determining the general principles of the common parliamentary law of the land, were it not for the fact that while the English Parliament has continued to be a strictly deliberative assembly, the business of our House of Representatives has grown so enormously that it has been obliged to make such changes in its rules and practice as will allow the majority to suppress the debate, if there has been previous debate, and if there has been none, to limit the debate to forty minutes; and also to suppress a question for the session even without any debate. These deviations from the old parliamentary law, while necessary in the House of Representatives, are in violation of the fundamental right of a deliberative assembly to have questions thoroughly discussed before it is called upon to take action upon them, unless a large majority, at least two-thirds, is prepared to act at once. In ordinary deliberative assemblies the right to debate questions before taking final action upon them should never be suppressed by less than a two-thirds vote, and the motion to lay on the table should be used only for its legitimate parliamentary purpose of laying aside a question temporarily.

Where the practice of Congress differs from that of Parliament, the common law of this country usually follows the practice of Congress. Thus, in every American deliberative assembly having no rules for conducting business, the motion to adjourn, when it does not dissolve the assembly, would be decided to be undebatable, as in Congress, the English parliamentary law to the contrary notwithstanding; so if the previous question were negatived, the debate upon the subject would continue, as in Congress, whereas in Parliament the subject would be immediately dismissed; so, too, the previous question could be moved when there was before the assembly a motion either to commit, or to postpone definitely or indefinitely, just as in Congress, notwithstanding that, according to English parliamentary law, the previous question could not be moved under such circumstances.

The old common parliamentary law gives the same rank to the motions for the previous question, to postpone definitely, to commit, and to postpone indefinitely, so that no one of them can be moved while another one of them is pending; the House makes them rank in the order just named; while the Senate does not admit the motion for the previous question, and makes to postpone indefinitely outrank all the others. The practice of the House in this matter establishes the parliamentary law of this country, as it does in all cases where its practice is not due to the great quantity of its business or the necessities of party government. This may be illustrated by the motions to lay on the table and the previous question. The House of Representatives has completely changed the use of the motion to lay on the table from that of merely laying aside a question until the assembly chooses to resume its consideration [see foot note, **28**], to a motion to kill the pending proposition. To make it more effective for this purpose, they have allowed it to be made before the member reporting a bill from the committee is allowed to speak, and when a question is laid upon the table it cannot be taken up except by suspending the rules, which requires a two-thirds vote. For reasons previously given, such rules are necessary in Congress, but in ordinary assemblies they would do more harm than good. The same vote should be required (two-thirds vote) to stop debate and bring the assembly to a vote on the final disposition of the question, whether the intention is to adopt or to reject the proposition. The previous question and the motion to lay on the table require the same vote in Congress, and should in all assemblies where to lay on the table is used for killing propositions.

The modifications made by the House in regard to the previous question have made that motion extremely simple and useful, and its practice establishes the parliamentary law of the country as to the previous question, except in respect to its being ordered by a majority vote and forty minutes' debate being allowed after it has been ordered, if the proposition has not been previously debated. It is necessary in Congress for the majority to have the power to close debate, but, such a power being in conflict with the fundamental rights of a deliberative assembly, Congress has modified it so as not to cut off debate entirely. In an ordinary assembly, with sessions not exceeding two or three hours, it should, and it does, have the power by a two-thirds vote to close debate instantly, just as by the same vote it may suspend the rules.

In matters of detail, the rules of the House of Representatives are adapted to the peculiar wants of that body, and are of no authority in any other assembly. No one, for instance, would accept the following House of Representatives rules as common parliamentary law in this country: That the chairman, in case of disorderly conduct, would have the power to order the galleries to be cleared; that any fifteen members would be authorized to compel the attendance of absent members; that each member would be limited in debate upon any question to one hour; and that the motion to suspend the rules can only be entertained on the first and third Mondays of each month. These examples are sufficient to show the absurdity of the idea that the rules of Congress in all things determine the common parliamentary law.

While some of the rules of Congress are adapted only to legislative assemblies, and others only to the House that adopts them, yet its rules and practice, except where manifestly unsuited to ordinary deliberative assemblies, should, and do determine the parliamentary law of the country. The people of the United States will never accept the rules and practice of the legislature, or of deliberative assemblies, of any state, or even of any section of the country, as of equal authority with the practice of the National Congress in determining the parliamentary law for the whole country.

Since, however, the sessions of Congress last from three to six months, and at times to nearly a year, whereas the great majority of ordinary deliberative assemblies have sessions lasting not more than two or three hours; and since the quorum in Congress is a majority of the members, while in most societies it is less than one-fifth, and often less than one-tenth, of the members; and since the members of Congress are paid to devote all their time during a session to the business of Congress, and can be compelled to attend, whereas in ordinary assemblies the members have other duties and their attendance is simply voluntary; and as the work of Congress is enormous and is mostly done by standing committees, of which there are fifty-six, or in committee of the whole, while in ordinary assemblies the assembly itself attends to most of its business, and the rest is done usually by special committees rather than by standing committees or in committee of the whole—as these differences exist, it is evident that the rules and practice of Congress require to be modified in some respects to adapt them to ordinary deliberative assemblies. Sometimes the old common parliamentary law is better adapted to ordinary societies, as with the motion to lay on the table. Where the two houses differ, sometimes the Senate practice is better adapted to ordinary assemblies, as in allowing each member to speak twice to the same question each day; while in allowing the previous question and in making the motion to postpone indefinitely the lowest of subsidiary motions, the practice of the House seems better adapted to ordinary assemblies. The House allows a majority to order the previous question, but if there has been no debate on the question, forty minutes' debate is permitted after the previous question has been ordered. This rule is not adapted to assemblies whose entire session may not last two hours. They should have power to close debate instantly by a two-thirds vote. This is in accordance with the general principle that the assembly by a two-thirds vote may suspend the rules, even the rule permitting debate.

As there would naturally be differences of opinion as to the application of the above principles, and it is important that the law should be definite, every deliberative assembly should imitate our legislative bodies and adopt some Rules of Order for the conduct of its business.*

PLAN OF THE WORK.

These Rules are prepared to meet partially this want in deliberative assemblies that are not legislative in their character. They have been made sufficiently complete to answer for the rules of an assembly until it sees fit to adopt special rules conflicting with and superseding any of the rules of detail, such as the Order of Business, etc. They are based upon the rules and practice of Congress so far as these are adapted to ordinary deliberative assemblies with short sessions and comparatively small quorums, as has just been explained. In cases where these Rules differ from the practice of Congress, usually the congressional rule will be found in a foot note. The foot notes need not be referred to for any other purpose than to ascertain the practice of Congress.

This Manual contains a Table of Contents, Table of Rules, Part I, Part II, Lesson Outlines, and the Index.

Table of Contents. This gives a clear, systematic idea of the arrangement of subjects treated in the Manual.

Order of Precedence of Motions and Table of Rules. A careful study of these tables so as to be able to use them quickly will enable any one in an emergency to ascertain whether a motion is in order, and whether it may be debated, or amended, or reconsidered, or requires a second, or a two-thirds vote, or is in order when another member has the floor.

Part I, comprising the main part of the Manual, contains a set of Rules of Order systematically arranged, as shown in the Table of Contents. It begins with showing how business is introduced in a deliberative assembly, and then follows it step by step until the vote is taken and announced. The next section,

---

* Any society adopting these Rules of Order should be governed by them in all cases to which they are applicable, and in which they are not inconsistent with the by-laws and rules of order of the society. [See p. 268 for the form of a rule covering this case.] Its own rules should include all of the cases where it is desirable to vary from the rules in the Manual, and especially should provide for a Quorum **[64]** and an Order of Business **[65]**, as suggested in this Manual.

10, shows what is the proper motion to use to accomplish certain objects, referring at the same time to the section where the motion will be found fully treated. Next, the motions are classified as usual into Privileged, Incidental, Subsidiary, and Main, and the general characteristics of each class given.

Then each class is taken up in order, beginning with the highest privileged motion, and a section is devoted to each motion, including some motions that are not classified. Each of these twenty-six sections is complete in itself, so that one unfamiliar with the work need not be misled in examining any particular subject. Cross-references, in heavy-face type, are used wherever it was thought they would be helpful, the references being to sections, the number of the section being placed at the top of each page. The following is stated in reference to each motion, except some of the incidental ones, the first six points being mentioned at the beginning of each section:

(1) Of what motions *it takes precedence* (that is, what motions may be pending and yet it be in order to make and consider this motion).

(2) To what motions *it yields* (that is, what motions may be made and considered while this motion is pending).

(3) Whether it is *debatable* or not (all motions being debatable unless the contrary is stated).

(4) Whether it can be *amended* or not.

(5) In case the motion can have no subsidiary motion *applied* to it, the fact is stated [see Adjourn, **17,** for an example: the meaning is, that the particular motion, to adjourn, cannot be laid on the table, postponed, committed, or amended, &c.].

(6) The *vote* required for its adoption, when it is not a majority.

(7) The *form of making the motion* when peculiar.

(8) The *form of stating and putting the question* when peculiar.

(9) The *object* of the motion when not apparent.

(10) The *effect* of the motion if adopted, whenever it could possibly be misunderstood.

Part II contains an explanation of the methods of organizing and conducting different kinds of meetings, giving the words used by the chairman and speakers in making and putting various motions; and also a few pages devoted to the legal rights of deliberative assemblies and ecclesiastical tribunals, and to the trial of members of such societies. The beginner, especially, will find it useful to read sections **69-71** in connection with sections **1-10**, thus obtaining correct ideas as to the methods of conducting business in deliberative assemblies.

The Plan for the Study of Parliamentary Law, pages 305-312, gives some helpful suggestions to clubs and individuals wishing to study parliamentary law, together with a series of eighteen Lesson Outlines.

The Index refers to pages, not sections, and at the beginning are given some suggestions as to the best method of finding anything in these Rules.

DEFINITIONS.

In addition to the terms defined above (*taking precedence of, yielding to,* and *applying to* [see p. 21]), there are other terms that are liable to be misunderstood, to which attention is called.

Accepting a report is the same as adopting it, and should not be confused with *receiving* a report, which is allowing it to be presented to the assembly.

Assembly. This term is used for the deliberative assembly, and should be replaced in motions, etc., by the proper name of the body, as society, club, church, board, convention, etc.

The *Chair* means the presiding officer, whether temporary or permanent.

The terms *Congress* and *H. R.*, when used in this Manual, refer to the U. S. House of Representatives.

Meeting and *Session.* Meeting is used in this Manual for an assembling of the members of a deliberative body for any length of time during which they do not separate for longer than a few minutes, as the morning meeting, or the evening meeting, of a convention. In a society with rules providing for regular meetings every week, or month, etc., each of these regular meetings is a separate session. A called or special meeting is a distinct session. Should a regular or special meeting adjourn to meet at another time, the adjourned meeting is a continuation of the session, not a separate one; the two meetings constitute one session. In the case of a convention holding a meeting every year or two, or rather a series of meetings lasting several days, the entire series of meetings constitute one session. [See **63.**]

Pending and *Immediately Pending.* A question is said to be pending when it has been stated by the chair and has not yet been disposed of either permanently or temporarily. When several questions are pending, the one last stated by the chair, and therefore the one to be first disposed of, is said to be the immediately pending question.

A *Main motion* is one that is made to bring before the assembly any particular subject. No main motion can be made when another motion is pending.

A *Subsidiary motion* is one that may be applied to a main motion, and to certain other motions, for the purpose of modifying them, delaying action upon them or otherwise disposing of them.

Privileged motions are such that, while having no relation to the pending question, are of such urgency or importance as to require them to take precedence of all other motions.

An *Incidental motion* is one that arises out of another question which is pending or has just been pending, and must be decided before the pending question, or before other business is taken up. Incidental motions have no fixed rank but take precedence of the questions out of which they arise, whether those questions are main or subsidiary or privileged.

The *Previous Question* does not refer, as its name would imply, to the previous question, but is the name given to the motion to close debate and at once to take the vote on the immediately pending question and such other questions as are specified in the motion.

A *Substitute* is an amendment where an entire resolution, or section, or one or more paragraphs, is struck out and another resolution, or section, or one or more paragraphs, is inserted in its place.

Plurality, Majority, and *Two-thirds* Vote. In an election a candidate has a plurality when he has a larger vote than any other candidate; he has a majority when he has more than half the votes cast, ignoring blanks. In an assembly a plurality never elects except by virtue of a rule to that effect. A majority vote when used in these rules means a majority of the votes cast, ignoring blanks, at a legal meeting, a quorum being present. A two-thirds vote is two-thirds of the votes just described. For an illustration of the difference between a two-thirds vote, a vote of two-thirds of the members present, and a vote of two-thirds of the members, see page 204.

TO THE READER.

The reader is advised to read this Manual in the order suggested in the Plan for the study of Parliamentary Law, page 305.

PART I.

RULES OF ORDER.

Art. I. How Business Is Conducted in Deliberative Assemblies.

1. **Introduction of Business.** An assembly having been organized as described in 69, 70, 71, business is brought before it either by the motion of a member, or by the presentation of a communication to the assembly. It is not usual to make motions to receive reports of committees or communications to the assembly. There are many other cases in the ordinary routine of business where the formality of a motion is dispensed with, but should

any member object, a regular motion becomes necessary, or the chair may put the question without waiting for a motion.

2. **What Precedes Debate.** Before any subject is open to debate it is necessary, first, that a motion be made by a member who has obtained the floor; second, that it be seconded (with certain exceptions); and third, that it be stated by the chair, that is, by the presiding officer. The fact that a motion has been made and seconded does not put it before the assembly, as the chair alone can do that. He must either rule it out of order, or state the question on it so that the assembly may know what is before it for consideration and action, that is, what is the *immediately pending question.* If several questions are pending, as a resolution and an amendment and a motion to postpone, the last one stated by the chair is the immediately pending question.

While no debate or other motion is in order after a motion is made, until it is stated or ruled out of order by the chair, yet members may suggest modifications of the motion, and the mover, without the consent of the seconder, has the right to make such modifications as he pleases, or even to withdraw his motion entirely before the chair states the question. After it is stated by the chair he can do neither without the consent of the assembly as shown in 27 (*c*). A little informal consultation before the question is stated often saves much time, but the chair must see that this privilege is not abused and allowed to run into debate. When the mover modifies his motion the one who seconded it has a right to withdraw his second.

3. Obtaining the Floor. Before a member can make a motion, or address the assembly in debate, it is necessary that he should *obtain the floor*—that is, he must rise after the floor has been yielded, and address the presiding officer by his official title, thus, "Mr. Chairman," or "Mr. President," or "Mr. Moderator;"* or, if a woman (married or single), "Madam Chairman," or "Madam President." If the assembly is large so that the member's name may be unknown to the chairman, the member should give his name as soon as he catches the eye of the chairman after addressing him. If the member is entitled to the floor, as shown hereafter, the chairman "recognizes" him, or assigns him the floor, by announcing his name. If the assembly is small and the members are known to each other, it is not necessary for the member to give his name after addressing the chair, as the presiding officer is termed, nor is it necessary for the chair to do more than bow in recognition of his having the floor. If a member rises before the floor has been yielded, or is standing at the time, he cannot obtain the floor pro-

* "Brother Moderator," or "Brother Chairman," implies that the speaker is also a moderator or chairman, and should not be used.

vided any one else rises afterwards and addresses the chair. It is out of order to be standing when another has the floor, and the one guilty of this violation of the rules cannot claim he rose first, as he did not rise after the floor had been yielded.

Where two or more rise about the same time to claim the floor, all other things being equal, the member who rose first after the floor had been yielded, and addressed the chair is entitled to the floor. It frequently occurs, however, that where more than one person claims the floor about the same time, the interests of the assembly require the floor to be assigned to a claimant that was not the first to rise and address the chair. There are three classes of such cases that may arise: (1) When a debatable question is immediately pending; (2) when an undebatable question is immediately pending; (3) when no question is pending. In such cases the chair in assigning the floor should be guided by the following principles:

(1) *When a Debatable Question is Immediately Pending.* (*a*) The member upon whose motion the immediately pending debatable question was brought before the assembly is entitled to be recognized as having the floor (if he has not already spoken on the question) even though another has risen first and addressed the chair. The member thus entitled to preference in recognition in case

of a committee's report is the reporting member (the one who presents or submits the report); in case of a question taken from the table, it is the one who moved to take the question from the table; in case of the motion to reconsider, it is the one who moved to reconsider, and who is not necessarily the one who calls up the motion. (*b*) No member who has already had the floor in debate on the immediately pending question is again entitled to it for debate on the same question, provided the floor is claimed by one who has not spoken on that question. (*c*) As the interests of the assembly are best subserved by allowing the floor to alternate between the friends and enemies of a measure, the chairman, when he knows which side of a question is taken by each claimant of the floor, and these claims are not determined by the above principles, should give the preference to the one opposed to the last speaker.

(2) *When an Undebatable Question Is Immediately Pending.* When the immediately pending question is undebatable, its mover has no preference to the floor, which should be assigned in accordance with the principles laid down under (*b*) in paragraph below.

(3) *When No Question Is Pending.* (*a*) When one of a series of motions has been disposed of, and there is no question actually pending, the next of the series has the right of way, and the chair should recognize the

member who introduced the series to make the next motion, even though another has risen first and addressed the chair. In fact no other main motion is in order until the assembly has disposed of the series. Thus, the motion to lay on the table, properly used, is designed to lay aside a question temporarily, in order to attend to some more urgent business, and, therefore, if a question is laid on the table, the one who moved to lay it on the table, if he immediately claims the floor, is entitled to it to introduce the urgent business even though another has risen first. So, when the rules are suspended to enable a motion to be made, the mover of the motion to suspend the rules is entitled to the floor to make the motion for which the rules were suspended, even though another rose first. When a member moves to reconsider a vote for the announced purpose of amending the motion, if the vote is reconsidered he must be recognized in preference to others in order to move his amendment. (*b*) If, when no question is pending and no series of motions has been started that has not been disposed of, a member rises to move to reconsider a vote, or to call up the motion to reconsider that had been previously made, or to take a question from the table when it is in order, he is entitled to the floor in preference to another that may have risen slightly before him to introduce a main motion, provided that when some one rises before him he, on rising, states the purpose for which he rises. If members, rising to make the above mentioned motions, come into competition they have the preference in the order in which these motions have just been given; first, to reconsider, and last, to take from the table. When a motion to appoint a committee for a certain purpose, or to refer a subject to a committee, has been adopted no new subject (except a privileged one) can be introduced until the assembly has decided all of the related questions as to the number of the committee, and as to how it shall be appointed, and as to any instructions to be given it. In this case the one who made the motion to appoint the committee or refer the subject to a committee has no preference in recognition. If he had wished to make the other motions he should have included them all in his first motion.

From the decision of the chair in assigning the floor any two members may appeal,* one making the appeal and the other seconding it. Where the chair is in doubt as to who is entitled to the floor, he may allow the assembly to decide the question by a vote, the one having the largest vote being entitled to the floor.

If a member has risen to claim the floor, or

---

* In the U. S. House of Representatives there is no appeal from the decision of the chair as to who is entitled to the floor, nor should there be any appeal in large mass meetings, as the best interests of the assembly require the chair to be given more power in such large bodies.

has been assigned the floor, and calls for the question are made, or it is moved to adjourn, or to lay the question on the table, it is the duty of the chair to suppress the disorder and protect the member who is entitled to the floor. Except by general consent, a motion cannot be made by one who has not been recognized by the chair as having the floor. If it is made it should not be recognized by the chair if any one afterwards rises and claims the floor, thus showing that general consent has not been given.

In Order When Another Has the Floor. After a member has been assigned the floor he cannot be interrupted by a member or the chairman, except by (*a*) a motion to reconsider; (*b*) a point of order; (*c*) an objection to the consideration of the question; (*d*) a call for the orders of the day when they are not being conformed to; (*e*) a question of privilege; (*f*) a request or demand that the question be divided when it consists of more than one independent resolution on different subjects; or (*g*) a parliamentary inquiry or a request for information that requires immediate answer; and these cannot interrupt him after he has actually commenced speaking unless the urgency is so great as to justify it. The speaker (that is, the member entitled to the floor) does not lose his right to the floor by these interruptions, and the interrupting member does not obtain the floor thereby, and after they have been attended to, the chair assigns him the floor again. So, when a member submitting a report from a committee or offering a resolution, hands it to the secretary to be read, he does not thereby yield his right to the floor. When the reading is finished and the chair states the question, neither the secretary nor any one else can make a motion until the member submitting the report, or offering the resolution, has had a reasonable opportunity to claim the floor to which he is entitled, and has not availed himself of his privilege. If, when he submitted the report, he made no motion to accept or adopt the recommendations or resolutions, he should resume the floor as soon as the report is read, and make the proper motion to carry out the recommendations, after which he is entitled to the floor for debate as soon as the question is stated.

4. Motions and Resolutions. A motion is a proposal that the assembly take certain action, or that it express itself as holding certain views. It is made by a member's obtaining the floor as already described and saying, "I move that" (which is equivalent to saying, "I propose that"), and then stating the action he proposes to have taken. Thus a member "moves" (proposes) that a resolution be adopted, or amended, or referred to a committee, or that a vote of thanks be extended, etc.; or "That it is the sense of this meeting (or assembly) that industrial training," etc. Every resolution should be in writing, and the presiding officer has a right to require any main motion, amendment, or instructions to a committee to be in writing. When a main motion is of such importance or length as to be in writing it is usually written in the form of a *resolution;* that is, beginning with the words, "*Resolved,* That," the word "*Resolved*" being underscored (printed in italics) and followed by a comma, and the word "That" beginning with a capital "T." If the word "Resolved" were replaced by the words "I move," the resolution would become a motion. A resolution is always a main motion. In some sections of the country the word "resolve" is frequently used instead of "resolution." In assemblies with paid employees, instructions given to employees are called "orders" instead of "resolutions," and the enacting word, "Ordered" is used instead of "Resolved."

When a member wishes a resolution adopted, after having obtained the floor, he says, "I move the adoption of the following resolution," or "I offer the following resolution," which he reads and hands to the chair. If it is desired to give the reasons for the resolution, they are usually stated in a *preamble,* each clause of which constitutes a paragraph beginning with "Whereas." The preamble is always amended last, as changes in the resolution may require changes in the preamble.

In moving the adoption of a resolution the preamble is not usually referred to, as it is included in the resolution. But when the previous question is ordered on the resolution before the preamble has been considered for amendment, it does not apply to the preamble, which is then open to debate and amendment. The preamble should never contain a period, but each paragraph should close with a comma or semicolon, followed by "and," except the last paragraph, which should close with the word "therefore," or "therefore, be it." A resolution should avoid periods where practicable. Usually, where periods are necessary, it is better to separate it into a series of resolutions, in which case the resolutions may be numbered, if preferred, by preceding them with the figures 1, 2, etc.; or it may retain the form of a single resolution with several paragraphs, each beginning with "That," and these may be numbered, if preferred, by placing "First," "Second," etc., just before the word "That." The following form will serve as a guide when it is desired to give the reasons for a resolution:

Whereas, We consider that suitable recreation is a necessary part of a rational educational system; and

Whereas, There is no public ground in this village where our school children can play; therefore,

Resolved, That it is the sense of this meeting that ample play grounds should be immediately provided for our school children.

Resolved, That a committee of five be appointed

by the chair to present these resolutions to the village authorities and to urge upon them prompt action in the matter.

As a general rule no member can make two motions at a time except by general consent. But he may combine the motion to suspend the rules with the motion for whose adoption it was made; and the motion to reconsider a resolution and its amendments; and a member may offer a resolution and at the same time move to make it a special order for a specified time.

5. **Seconding Motions.** As a general rule, with the exceptions given below, every motion should be seconded. This is to prevent time being consumed in considering a question that only one person favors, and consequently little attention is paid to it in routine motions. Where the chair is certain the motion meets with general favor, and yet members are slow about seconding it, he may proceed without waiting for a second. Yet, any one may make a point of order that the motion has not been seconded, and then the chair is obliged to proceed formally and call for a second. The better way when a motion is not at once seconded, is for the chair to ask, "Is the motion seconded?" In a very large hall the chair should repeat the motion before calling for a second in order that all may hear. After a motion has been made no other motion is in order until the chair has stated the

question on this motion, or has declared, after a reasonable opportunity has been given for a second, that the motion has not been seconded, or has ruled it out of order. Except in very small assemblies the chair cannot assume that members know what the motion is and that it has not been seconded, unless he states the facts.

A motion is seconded by a member's saying, "I second the motion," or "I second it," which he does without obtaining the floor, and in small assemblies without rising. In large assemblies, and especially where non-members are scattered throughout the assembly, members should rise, and without waiting for recognition, say, "Mr. Chairman, I second the motion."

Exceptions. The following do not require a second:*

Question of Privilege, to raise a............ 19
Questions of Order........................ 21
Objection to the Consideration of a Question 23
Call for Orders of the Day............... 20
Call for Division of the Question (under certain circumstances)..................... 24
Call for Division of the Assembly (in voting) 25
Call up Motion to Reconsider............. 36
Filling Blanks............................ 33
Nominations 33
Leave to Withdraw a Motion.............. 27
Inquiries of any kind..................... 27

* In Congress motions are not required to be seconded.

6. Stating the Question. When a motion has been made and seconded, it is the duty of the chair, unless he rules it out of order, immediately to *state the question*—that is, state the exact question that is before the assembly for its consideration and action. This he may do in various ways, depending somewhat on the nature of the question, as illustrated by the following examples: "It is moved and seconded that the following resolution be adopted [reading the resolution];" or "It is moved and seconded to adopt the following resolution;" "Mr. A offers the following resolution [read]: the question is on its adoption;" "It is moved and seconded to amend the resolution by striking out the word 'very' before the word 'good';" "The previous question has been demanded [or, moved and seconded] on the amendment;" "It is moved and seconded that the question be laid on the table;" "It is moved and seconded that we adjourn." [Under each motion is shown the form of stating the question if there is any peculiarity in the form.] If the question is debatable or amendable, the chair should immediately ask, "Are you ready for the question?" If no one then rises he should put the question as described in 9. If the question cannot be debated or amended, he does not ask, "Are you ready for the question?" but immediately puts the question after stating it.

7. Debate. After a question has been

stated by the chair, it is before the assembly for consideration and action. All resolutions, reports of committees, communications to the assembly, and all amendments proposed to them, and all other motions except the Undebatable Motions mentioned in **45**, may be debated before final action is taken on them, unless by a two-thirds vote the assembly decides to dispose of them without debate. By a two-thirds vote is meant two-thirds of the votes cast, a quorum being present. In the debate each member has the right to speak twice on the same question on the same day (except on an appeal), but cannot make a second speech on the same question as long as any member who has not spoken on that question desires the floor. No one can speak longer than ten minutes at a time without permission of the assembly.

Debate must be limited to the merits of the *immediately pending question*—that is, the last question stated by the chair that is still pending; except that in a few cases the main question is also open to debate [**45**]. Speakers must address their remarks to the presiding officer, be courteous in their language and deportment, and avoid all personalities, never alluding to the officers or other members by name, where possible to avoid it, nor to the motives of members. [For further information on this subject see Debate, **42**, and Decorum in Debate, **43**.]

8. Secondary Motions. To assist in the proper disposal of the question various *subsidiary* [12] motions are used, such as to amend, to commit, etc., and for the time being the subsidiary motion replaces the resolution, or motion, and becomes the immediately pending question. While these are pending, a question incidental to the business may arise, as a question of order, and this *incidental* [13] question interrupts the business and, until disposed of, becomes the immediately pending question. And all of these may be superseded by certain motions, called *privileged* [14] motions, as to adjourn, of such supreme importance as to justify their interrupting all other questions. All of these motions that may be made while the original motion is pending are sometimes referred to as *secondary* motions. The proper use of many of these is shown in **10**.

9. Putting the Question and Announcing the Vote.* When the debate appears to have closed, the chair asks again, "Are you ready for the question?" If no one rises he

* H. R. Rule 1, §5, is as follows: "5. He shall rise to put a question, but may state it sitting; and shall put questions in this form, to wit: 'As many as are in favor (as the question may be), say *Aye;*' and after the affirmative voice is expressed, 'As many as are opposed, say *No;*' if he doubts, or a division is called for, the House shall divide; those in the affirmative of the question shall first rise from their seats, and then those in the negative; if he still doubts, or a count is required by at least one-fifth of a quorum, he shall name one from each side of the question to tell the members in the affirmative and negative; which being reported, he shall rise and state the decision."

proceeds to *put the question*—that is, to take the vote on the question, first calling for the affirmative and then for the negative vote. In putting the question the chair should make perfectly clear what the question is that the assembly is to decide. If the question is on the adoption of a resolution, unless it has been read very recently, it should be read again, the question being put in a way similar to this: "The question is on the adoption of the resolution [which the chair reads]; those in favor of the resolution say *aye;* those opposed say *no.* The ayes have it, and the resolution is adopted;" or, "The noes have it, and the resolution is lost." Or, thus: "The question is on agreeing to the following resolution," which the chair reads, and then he continues, "As many as are in favor of agreeing to the resolution say *aye*;" after the ayes have responded he continues, "As many as are opposed say *no*. The ayes have it," etc. Or, "It is moved and seconded that an invitation be extended to Mr. Jones to address our club at its next meeting. Those in favor of the motion will rise; be seated; those opposed will rise. The affirmative has it and the motion is adopted [or carried]." Or, if the vote is by "show of hands," the question is put and the vote announced in a form similar to this: "It has been moved and seconded to lay the resolution on the table. Those in favor of the motion will raise the right hand; those opposed will signify [or manifest] it in the same way [or manner]. The affirmative has it [or, The motion is adopted, or carried] and the resolution is laid on the table." The vote should always be announced, as it is a necessary part of putting the question. The assembly is assumed not to know the result of the vote until announced by the chair, and the vote does not go into effect until announced. As soon as the result of the vote is announced the chair should state the next business in order, as in the following example of putting the question on an amendment: "The question is on amending the resolution by inserting the word 'oak' before the word 'desk.' Those in favor of the amendment say *aye;* those opposed say *no.* The ayes have it and the amendment is adopted. The question is now [or recurs] on the resolution as amended, which is as follows: [read the resolution as amended]. Are you ready for the question?" The chair should never neglect to state what is the business next in order after every vote is announced, nor to state the exact question before the assembly whenever a motion is made. Much confusion is avoided thereby. The vote should always be taken first by the voice (viva voce) or by show of hands (the latter method being often used in small assemblies), except in the case of motions requiring a two-thirds vote, when a rising vote should be taken at first. When a division is demanded a rising vote is taken. For further information on voting see **46.** Under each motion is given the form of putting the question whenever the form is peculiar.

10. Proper Motions to Use to Accomplish Certain Objects. To enable any one to ascertain what motion to use in order to accomplish what is desired, the common motions are arranged in the table below according to the objects to be attained by their use. Immediately after the table is a brief statement of the differences between the motions placed under each object, and of the circumstances under which each should be used. They include all of the Subsidiary Motions [**12**], which are designed for properly disposing of a question pending before the assembly; and the three motions designed to again bring before the assembly a question that has been acted upon or laid aside temporarily; and the motion designed to bring before another meeting of the assembly a main question which has been voted on in an unusually small or unrepresentative meeting. Motions, as a general rule, require for their adoption only a majority vote—that is, a majority of the votes cast, a quorum being present; but motions to suppress or limit debate, or to prevent the consideration of a question, or, without notice to rescind action previously taken, require a two-thirds vote [**48**]. The figures and letters on the left in the list below correspond to similar figures and letters in the statement of differences further on. The figures to the right in the list refer to the sections where the motions are fully treated.

The Common Motions Classified According to Their Objects.

(1) To Modify or Amend.
- (*a*) *Amend* 33
- (*b*) *Commit or Refer*................ 32

(2) To Defer Action.
- (*a*) *Postpone to a Certain Time*...... 31
- (*b*) *Make a Special Order* (2/3 Vote) 20
- (*c*) *Lay on the Table*............... 28

(3) To Suppress or Limit Debate (2/3 Vote).
- (*a*) *Previous Question* (*to close debate now*) (2/3 Vote)............. 29
- (*b*) *Limit Debate* (2/3 Vote)........ 30

(4) To Suppress the Question.
- (*a*) *Objection to Its Consideration* (2/3 Vote)..................... 23
- (*b*) *Previous Question and Reject Question* 29
- (*c*) *Postpone Indefinitely*........... 34
- (*d*) *Lay on the Table*............... 28

(5) To Consider a Question a Second Time.
- (*a*) *Take from the Table*........... 35
- (*b*) *Reconsider* 36
- (*c*) *Rescind* 37

(6) To Prevent Final Action on a Question in an Unusually Small or Unrepresentative Meeting.
- (*a*) *Reconsider and have Entered on the Minutes* 36

(1) *To Modify or Amend.* (*a*) When a resolution or motion is not worded properly, or requires any modification to meet the ap-

proval of the assembly, if the changes required can be made in the assembly, the proper motion to make is to *amend* by "inserting," or "adding," or by "striking out," or by "striking out and inserting," or by "substituting" one or more paragraphs for those in the resolution. (*b*) But if much time will be required, or if the changes required are numerous, or if additional information is required to enable the assembly to act intelligently, then it is usually better *to refer* the question to a committee.

(2) *To Defer Action.* (*a*) If it is desired to put off the further consideration of a question to a certain hour, so that when that time arrives, as soon as the pending business is disposed of, it shall have the right of consideration over all questions except special orders and a reconsideration, then the proper motion to make is, *to postpone to that certain time.* This is also the proper motion to make if it is desired to defer action simply to another day. As the motion if adopted cannot interrupt the pending question when the appointed time arrives, nor can it suspend any rule, it requires only a majority vote for its adoption. A question postponed to a certain time cannot be taken up before the appointed time except by suspending the rules, which requires a two-thirds vote. (*b*) If it is desired to appoint for the consideration of a question a certain time when it may interrupt any pending question except one relating to

adjournment or recess, or a question of privilege or a specified order that was made before it was, then the proper course is to move "that the question be made a *special order* for," etc., specifying the day or hour. As this motion, if adopted, suspends all rules that interfere with the consideration of the question at the appointed time, it requires a two-thirds vote for its adoption. A special order cannot be considered before the appointed time except by suspending the rules, which requires a two-thirds vote. (*c*) If, however, it is desired to lay the question aside temporarily with the right to take it up at any moment when business of this class, or unfinished or new business, is in order and no other question is before the assembly, the proper motion to use is to *lay the question on the table*. When laid upon the table a majority vote may take it up at the same or the next session, as described in 35.

(3) *To Suppress Debate.* (*a*) If it is desired to close debate now and bring the assembly at once to a vote on the pending question, or questions, the proper course is to move, or demand, or call for, the previous question on the motions upon which it is desired to close debate. The motion, or demand, for the previous question should always specify the motions upon which it is desired to order the previous question. If no motions are specified, the previous question applies only

to the immediately pending question. It requires a two-thirds vote for its adoption. After it has been adopted, privileged and incidental motions may be made, or the pending questions may be laid on the table, but no other subsidiary motion can be made nor is any debate allowed. If it is lost the debate is resumed. (*b*) If it is desired to limit the number or length of speeches, or the time allowed for debate, the proper course is to move that the speeches or debate be limited as desired, or that the debate be closed and the vote be taken at a specified time. These motions to limit or close debate require a two-thirds vote for their adoption, and are in order, like the previous question, when any debatable question is immediately pending.

(4) *To Suppress the Question.* A legitimate question cannot be suppressed in a deliberative assembly without free debate, except by a two-thirds vote. If two-thirds of the assembly are opposed to the consideration of the question then it can be suppressed by the following methods: (*a*) If it is desired to prevent any consideration of the question, the proper course to pursue is *to object to its consideration* before it has been discussed or any other motion stated, and, therefore, it may interrupt a member who has the floor before the debate has begun. It requires no second. On the question of consideration there must be a two-thirds negative vote to

prevent the consideration. (*b*) After the question has been considered the proper way to immediately suppress it is to close debate by ordering the *previous question,* which requires a two-thirds vote, and then to vote down the question. (*c*) Another method of suppressing a question is to *postpone it indefinitely* (equivalent to rejecting it), which, however, being debatable and opening the main question to debate, is only of service in giving another opportunity to defeat the resolution should this one fail. For, if the motion to postpone indefinitely is adopted, the main question is dead for that session, and if it is lost, the main question is still pending and its enemies have another opportunity to kill it. When the motion to postpone indefinitely is pending and immediate action is desired, it is necessary to move the previous question as in case (*b*) above. (*d*) A fourth method frequently used for suppressing a question is to *lay it on the table,* though this is an unfair use of the motion, except in bodies like Congress where the majority must have the power to suppress any motion immediately, as otherwise they could not transact business. But in ordinary societies, where the pressure of business is not so great, it is better policy for the majority to be fair and courteous to the minority and use the proper motions for suppressing a question without allowing full debate, all of which require a two-thirds vote. Unless the enemies of a motion have a large majority, laying it on the table is not a safe way of suppressing it, because its friends, by watching their opportunity, may find themselves in a majority and take it from the table and adopt it, as shown in the next paragraph.

(5) *To Consider a Question a Second Time.* (*a*) When a question has not been voted on, but has been laid on the table, a majority may *take it from the table* and consider it at any time when no other question is before the assembly and when business of that class, or unfinished or new business, is in order during the same session; or at the next session in ordinary societies having regular meetings as often as quarterly. (*b*) If a motion has been adopted, or rejected, or postponed indefinitely, and afterwards one or more members have changed their views from the prevailing to the losing side, and it is thought that by further discussion the assembly may modify or reverse its action, the proper course is for one who voted with the prevailing side to move to *reconsider* the vote on the question. This can be done on the day the vote to be reconsidered is taken, or on the next succeeding day of the same session. (*c*) If a main motion, including questions of privilege and orders of the day, has been adopted or rejected or postponed indefinitely, and no one is both able and willing to move to reconsider the vote, the question can be brought up again

during the same session only by moving to *rescind* the motion. To rescind may be moved by any member, but, if notice of it was not given at a previous meeting, it requires a two-thirds vote or a vote of a majority of the enrolled membership. At any future session, the resolution, or other main motion, may be rescinded in the same way if it had been adopted; or it may be introduced anew if it had been rejected or postponed indefinitely; provided the question cannot be reached by calling up the motion to reconsider which had been made at the previous session. A by-law, or anything else that requires a definite notice and vote for its amendment, requires the same notice and vote to rescind it.

(6) *To Prevent Final Action on a Question in an Unusually Small or Unrepresentative Meeting.* If an important main motion should be adopted, lost, or postponed indefinitely, at a small or unrepresentative meeting of the society when it was apparent that the action is in opposition to the views of the majority of the members, the proper course to pursue is for a member to vote with the prevailing side and then move to reconsider the vote and have it entered on the minutes. The motion to reconsider, in this form, can be made only on the day the vote was taken which it is proposed to reconsider, and the reconsideration cannot be called up on that

day; thus an opportunity is given to notify absent members. The motion to reconsider is fully explained in 36.

Art. II. General Classification of Motions.

For convenience motions may be classified as follows:

11. A Main or Principal Motion is a motion made to bring before the assembly, for its consideration, any particular subject. It takes precedence of nothing—that is, it cannot be made when any other question is before the assembly; and it yields to all Privileged, Incidental, and Subsidiary Motions—that is, any of these motions can be made while a main motion is pending. Main motions are debatable, and subject to amendment, and can have any subsidiary [12] motions applied to them. When a main motion is laid on the table, or postponed to a certain time, it carries with it all pending subsidiary motions. If a main motion is referred to a committee it carries with it only the pending amendments. As a general rule, they require for their adoption only a majority vote—that is, a majority of the votes cast; but amendments to constitutions, by-laws, and rules of order already adopted, all of which are main motions, require a two-thirds vote for their adoption, unless the by-laws, etc., specify a different vote for their amendment; and the motion to rescind action previously taken requires a two-thirds vote, or a vote of a majority of the entire membership, unless previous notice of the motion has been given.

Main motions may be subdivided into Original Main Motions and Incidental Main Motions. *Original Main Motions* are those which bring before the assembly some new subject, generally in the form of a resolution, upon which action by the assembly is desired. *Incidental Main Motions* are those main motions that are incidental to, or relate to, the business of the assembly, or its past or future action, as, a committee's report on a resolution referred to it. A motion to accept or adopt the report of a standing committee upon a subject not referred to it is an original main motion, but a motion to adopt a report on a subject referred to a committee is an incidental main motion. The introduction of an original main motion can be prevented by sustaining by a two-thirds vote an objection to its consideration [23], made just after the main motion is stated and before it is discussed. An objection to its consideration cannot be applied to an incidental main motion, but a two-thirds vote can immediately suppress it by ordering the previous question [29]. This is the only difference between the two classes of main motions. The following list contains some of the most common

Incidental Main Motions.

All of these motions are essentially main motions, and are treated as such, though they may appear otherwise.

Though a question of privilege is of high rank so far as interrupting a pending question is concerned, yet when the question has interrupted business and is pending, it is treated as a main motion so far as having incidental and subsidiary motions applied to it. So an order of the day, even though a special order, after it has been taken up is treated in the same way, as is also a question that has been reconsidered.

No motion is in order that conflicts with the constitution, by-laws, or standing rules or resolutions of the assembly, and if such a motion is adopted it is null and void. Before introducing such a motion it is necessary to amend the constitution or by-laws, or amend or rescind the conflicting standing rule or resolution. So, too, a motion is not in order that conflicts with a resolution previously adopted by the assembly at the same session, or that has been introduced and has not been finally disposed of. If it is not too late the proper course is to reconsider [36] the vote on the motion previously adopted, and then amend it so as to express the desired idea. If it cannot be reconsidered, then by a two-thirds vote the old resolution may be rescinded when the new one can be introduced, or by giving notice it may be rescinded by a majority vote at the next meeting. In ordinary societies, where the quorum is a small percentage of the membership, and the meetings are as frequent as quarterly, no resolution that conflicts with one adopted at a previous session should be entertained until the old one has been rescinded, which requires a two-thirds vote unless proper notice has been given. [See 37.]

12. Subsidiary Motions are such as are applied to other motions for the purpose of most appropriately disposing of them. By means of them the original motion may be modified, or action postponed, or it may be referred to a committee to investigate and report, etc. They may be applied to any main motion, and when made they supersede the main motion and must be decided before the main motion can be acted upon. None of them, except the motion to amend and those that close or limit or extend the limits of debate, can be applied to a subsidiary, incidental (except an appeal in certain cases), or privileged motion. Subsidiary motions, except to lay on the table, the previous question, and postpone indefinitely, may be amended. The motions affecting the limits of debate may be applied to any debatable question regardless of its privilege, and require a two-thirds vote for their adoption. All those of lower rank than those affecting the limits of debate are debatable; the rest are not. The motion to amend anything that has already been adopted, as by-laws or minutes, is not a subsidiary motion but is a main motion and can be laid on the table or have applied to it any other subsidiary motion without affecting the by-laws or minutes, because the latter are not pending.

In the following list the subsidiary motions are arranged in the order of their precedence, the first one having the highest rank. When one of them is the immediately pending question every motion above it is in order, and every one below it is out of order. They are as follows:

Subsidiary Motions.

13. Incidental Motions are such as arise out of another question which is pending, and therefore take precedence of and must be decided before the question out of which they rise; or, they are incidental to a question that has just been pending and should be decided before any other business is taken up. They yield to privileged motions, and generally to the motion to lay on the table. They are undebatable, except an appeal under certain circumstances as shown in 21. They cannot be amended except where they relate to the division of a question, or to the method of considering a question, or to methods of voting, or to the time when nominations or the polls shall be closed. No subsidiary motion, except to amend, can be applied to any of them except a debatable appeal. Whenever it is stated that all incidental motions take precedence of a certain motion, the incidental motions referred to are only those that are legitimately incidental at the time they are made. Thus, incidental motions take precedence of subsidiary motions, but the incidental motion to object to the consideration of a question cannot be made while a subsidiary motion is pending, as the objection is only legitimate against an original main motion just after it is stated, before it has been debated or there has been any subsidiary motion stated. The following list comprises most of those that may arise:

Incidental Motions.

14. **Privileged Motions** are such as, while not relating to the pending question, are of so great importance as to require them to take precedence of all other questions, and, on account of this high privilege, they are undebatable. They cannot have any subsidiary

motion applied to them, except the motions to fix the time to which to adjourn, and to take a recess, which may be amended. But after the assembly has actually taken up the orders of the day or a question of privilege, debate and amendment are permitted and the subsidiary motions may be applied the same as on any main motion. These motions are as follows, being arranged in order of precedence:

Privileged Motions.

Fix the Time to which to Adjourn (if made while another question is pending)........ **16**
Adjourn (if unqualified and if it has not the effect to dissolve the assembly)........... **17**
Take a Recess (if made when another question is pending)......................... **18**
Raise a Question of Privilege.............. **19**
Call for Orders of the Day................ **20**

15. Some Main and Unclassified Motions. Two main motions (to rescind and to ratify) and several motions which cannot conveniently be classified as either Main, Subsidiary, Incidental, or Privileged, and which are in common use, are hereafter explained and their privileges and effects given. They are as follows:

Take from the Table...................... **35**
Reconsider **36**
Rescind **37**
Renewal of a Motion...................... **38**
Ratify **39**
Dilatory, Absurd, or Frivolous Motions..... **40**
Call of the House......................... **41**

Art. III. Privileged Motions.

See 14 for a list and the general characteristics of these motions.

16. To Fix the Time to which the Assembly shall Adjourn.* This motion is privileged only when made while another question is pending and in an assembly that has made no provision for another meeting on the same or the next day. The time fixed cannot be beyond the time of the next meeting. If made in an assembly that already has provided for another meeting on the same or the next day, or if made in an assembly when no question is pending, this is a main motion and may be debated and amended and have applied to it the other subsidiary motions, like other main motions. Whenever the motion is referred to in these rules the privileged motion is meant, unless specified to the contrary.

This motion when privileged takes precedence of all others, and is in order even after it has been voted to adjourn, provided the chairman has not declared the assembly adjourned. It can be amended, and a vote on it can be reconsidered. When the assembly

* In Congress this motion was given the highest rank of all motions, but it was so utilized for filibustering purposes and there was so little need of such a motion in an assembly meeting daily for months, that in the last revision of the rules it was omitted from the list of privileged motions. In ordinary assemblies having short or infrequent sessions its usefulness outweighs the harm that may be done by its improper use.

has no fixed place for its meetings, this motion should include the place as well as the time for the next meeting, and in this case the place is subject to amendment as well as the time. When the assembly meets at the time to which it adjourned, the meeting is a continuation of the previous session. Thus, if the Annual Meeting is adjourned to meet on another day, the adjourned meeting is a legal continuation of the Annual Meeting. [See 63.] The form of this motion is, "I move that when we adjourn, we adjourn (or stand adjourned) to 2 P. M. tomorrow."

17. To Adjourn. The motion to adjourn (when unqualified) is always a privileged motion except when, for lack of provision for a future meeting, as in a mass meeting, or at the last meeting of a convention, its effect, if adopted, would be to dissolve the assembly permanently. In any organized society holding several regular meetings during the year, it is, when unqualified, always a privileged motion. When not privileged it is treated as any other main motion, being debatable and amendable, etc.

The privileged motion to adjourn takes precedence of all others, except the privileged motion "to fix the time to which to adjourn," to which it yields. It is not debatable, nor can it be amended or have any other subsidiary [12] motion applied to it; nor can a vote on it be reconsidered. It may be withdrawn.

The motion to adjourn can be repeated if there has been any intervening business, though it is simply progress in debate. The assembly may decline to adjourn in order to hear one speech or to take one vote, and therefore it must have the privilege of renewing the motion to adjourn when there has been any progress in business or debate. But this high privilege is liable to abuse to the annoyance of the assembly, if the chair does not prevent it by refusing to entertain the motion when evidently made for obstructive purposes, as when the assembly has just voted it down, and nothing has occurred since to show the possibility of the assembly's wishing to adjourn. [See Dilatory Motions, 40.]

The motion to adjourn, like every other motion, cannot be made except by a member who has the floor. When made by one who has not risen and addressed the chair and been recognized, it can be entertained only by general consent. It cannot be made when the assembly is engaged in voting, or verifying the vote, but is in order after the vote has been taken by ballot before it has been announced. In such case the ballot vote should be announced as soon as business is resumed. Where much time will be consumed in counting ballots the assembly may adjourn, having previously appointed a time for the next meeting, or, still better, may take a recess as explained in the next section. No appeal, or question of order, or inquiry, should be entertained after the motion to adjourn has been made, unless it is of such a nature that its decision is necessary before an adjournment, or unless the assembly refuses to adjourn, when it would be in order.

Before putting the motion to adjourn, the chair, in most organizations, should be sure that no important matters have been overlooked. If there are announcements to be made they should be attended to before taking the vote, or at least, before announcing it. If there is something requiring action before adjournment, the fact should be stated and the mover requested to withdraw his motion to adjourn. The fact that the motion to adjourn is undebatable does not prevent the assembly's being informed of business requiring attention before adjournment. Members should not leave their seats until the chair has declared the assembly adjourned.

An adjournment sine die—that is, without day—closes the session and if there is no provision for convening the assembly again, of course the adjournment dissolves the assembly. But, if any provision has been made whereby another meeting may be held, its effect is simply to close the session. In an assembly, as a convention, which meets regularly only once during its life, but whose bylaws provide for calling special meetings, an adjournment sine die means only the ending of the regular session of the convention, which, however, may be reconvened as provided in the by-laws. If called to meet again the assembly meets as a body already organized.

When the motion to adjourn is qualified in any way, or when its effect is to dissolve the assembly without any provision being made for holding another meeting of the assembly, it loses its privilege and is a main motion, debatable and amendable and subject to having applied to it any of the subsidiary motions.

In committees where no provision has been made for future meetings, an adjournment is always at the call of the chair unless otherwise specified. When a special committee, or the committee of the whole, has completed the business referred to it, instead of adjourning, it *rises* and reports, which is equivalent to adjournment without day.

The *Effect upon Unfinished Business* of an adjournment, unless the assembly has adopted rules to the contrary, is as follows:

(*a*) When the adjournment does not close the session [63], the business interrupted by it is the first in order after the reading of the minutes at the next meeting, and is treated the same as if there had been no adjournment, an adjourned meeting being legally the continuation of the meeting of which it is an adjournment.

(*b*) When the adjournment closes a session* in an assembly having regular sessions as often as quarterly, the unfinished business should be taken up, just where it was interrupted at the next succeeding session previous to new business; provided that, in a body elected, either wholly or in part, for a definite time (as a board of directors one-third of whom are elected annually), unfinished business falls to the ground with the expiration of the term for which the board, or any part of it, was elected.

(*c*) When the adjournment closes a session in an assembly which does not meet as often as quarterly, or when the assembly is an elective body, and this session ends the term of a portion of the members, the adjournment puts an end to all business unfinished at the close of the session. The business may be introduced at the next session, the same as if it had never been before the assembly.

18. Take a Recess.† This motion is practically a combination of the two preceding, to

---

* "All business before committees of the House at the end of one session shall be resumed at the commencement of the next session of the same Congress in the same manner as if no adjournment had taken place." H. R. Rule 26. In practice this rule is applied to business before the House as well as to that before committees. But unfinished business does not go over from one Congress to another Congress. When a society meets only once in six months or a year, there is liable to be as great a difference in the personnel of the two consecutive meetings as of two consecutive Congresses; and only trouble would result from allowing unfinished business to hold over to the next yearly meeting.

† Congress has omitted this motion from its latest revision of the list of privileged motions, on account of its abuse for filibustering purposes, and its being so seldom needed.

which it yields, taking precedence of all other motions. If made when other business is before the assembly, it is a privileged motion and is undebatable and can have no subsidiary motion applied to it except amend. It can be amended as to the length of the recess. It takes effect immediately. A motion to take a recess made when no business is before the assembly, or a motion to take a recess at a future time, has no privilege, and is treated as any other main motion. A recess is an intermission in the day's proceedings, as for meals or for counting the ballots when much time is required; or in the case of meetings like conventions lasting for several days a recess is sometimes taken over an entire day. When a recess is provided for in the order of exercises, or program, the chair, when the time arrives, announces the fact and says the assembly stands adjourned, or in recess, to the specified hour. The assembly by a two-thirds vote can postpone the time for taking a recess, or adjournment. When the hour has arrived to which the recess was taken, the chairman calls the assembly to order and the business proceeds the same as if no recess had been taken. If the recess was taken after a vote had been taken and before it was announced, then the first business is the announcement of the vote. The intermissions in the proceedings of a day are termed recesses, whether the assembly voted to take a recess, or whether it simply adjourned having previously adopted a program or rule providing for the hours of meeting. When an assembly has frequent short regular meetings not lasting over a day, and an adjourned meeting is held on another day, the interval between the meetings is not referred to as a recess.

19. **Questions of Privilege.** Questions relating to the rights and privileges of the assembly, or to any of its members, take precedence of all other motions except the three preceding relating to adjournment and recess, to which they yield. If the question is one requiring immediate action it may interrupt a member's speech; as, for example, when, from any cause, a report that is being read cannot be heard in a part of the hall. But if it is not of such urgency it should not interrupt a member after he has commenced his speech. Before a member has commenced speaking, even though he has been assigned the floor, it is in order for another member to raise a question of privilege. When a member rises for this purpose he should not wait to be recognized, but immediately on rising should say, "Mr. Chairman,"—and when he catches the chairman's eye, should add, "I rise to a question of privilege affecting the assembly," or "I rise to a question of personal privilege." The chair directs him to state his question, and then decides whether

it is one of privilege or not. From this decision any two members may appeal. The chair may decide it to be a question of privilege, but not of sufficient urgency to justify interrupting the speaker. In such a case the speaker should be allowed to continue, and, when he has finished, the chair should immediately assign the floor to the member who raised the question of privilege to make his motion if one is necessary. Whenever his motion is made and stated, it becomes the immediately pending question and is open to debate and amendment and the application of all the other subsidiary motions just as any main motion. Its high privilege extends only to giving it the right to consideration in preference to any other question except one relating to adjournment or recess, and, in cases of great urgency, the right to interrupt a member while speaking. It cannot interrupt voting or verifying a vote. As soon as the question of privilege is disposed of, the business is resumed exactly where it was interrupted; if a member had the floor at the time the question of privilege was raised, the chair assigns him the floor again.

Questions of privilege may relate to the privileges of the assembly or only of a member, the former having the precedence if the two come into competition. Questions of personal privilege must relate to one as a member of the assembly, or else relate to charges against his character which, if true, would incapacitate him for membership. Questions like the following relate to the privileges of the assembly: those relating to the organization of the assembly; or to the comfort of its members, as the heating, lighting, ventilation, etc., of the hall, and freedom from noise and other disturbance; or to the conduct of its officers or employees; or to the punishing of a member for disorderly conduct or other offence; or to the conduct of reporters for the press, or to the accuracy of published reports of proceedings.

Privileged questions include, besides questions of privilege, a call for the orders of the day and the privileged motions relating to adjournment and recess. This distinction between privileged questions and questions of privilege should be borne in mind.

20. Orders of the Day.* *A Call for the Orders of the Day* (which, in an ordinary assembly, is a demand that the assembly conform to its program or order of business) can be made at any time when no other privileged [14] motion is pending and the order of business is being varied from, and only then. It requires no second, and is in order when another has the floor, even though it

---

* While Congress retains the call for the orders of the day in its list of privileged motions, it has abandoned the use of orders of the day, having, instead, a detailed order of business with several calendars. It retains special orders which may be made by a two-thirds vote.

interrupts a speech, as a single member has a right to demand that the order of business be conformed to. It is out of order to call for the orders of the day when there is no variation from the order of business. Thus, the orders of the day cannot be called for when another question is pending, provided there are no special orders made for that time or an earlier time, as general orders cannot interrupt a question actually under consideration. The call must be simply for the orders of the day, and not for a specified one, as the latter has no privilege. When the time has arrived for which a special order has been made, a call for the orders of the day takes precedence of everything except the other privileged motions, namely, those relating to adjournment and recess, and questions of privilege, to which it yields. If there are no special orders a call for the orders of the day cannot interrupt a pending question; but, if made when no question is pending, it is in order even when another has the floor and has made a main motion, provided the chair has not stated the question. Until the time of actually taking up the general orders for consideration this call yields to a motion to reconsider, or to a calling up of a motion to reconsider, previously made. A call for the orders of the day cannot be debated or amended, or have any other subsidiary motion applied to it.

It is the duty of the chair to announce the business to come before the assembly in its proper order, and if he always performs this duty there will be no occasion for calling for the orders of the day. But there are occasions when the chair fails to notice that the time assigned for a special order has arrived, or he thinks that the assembly is so interested in the pending question that it does not wish yet to take up the special order assigned for that time, and therefore delays announcing it. In such a case, as already stated, any member has a right to call for the orders of the day, and thus compel the chair either to announce the order or else put the question, "Will the assembly proceed to the orders of the day?" To refuse to take up the orders at the appointed time is an interference with the order of business similar to suspending the rules and should require the same vote—namely, two-thirds. In other words, a two-thirds vote in the negative is necessary to prevent proceeding to the orders of the day. If the assembly refuses to proceed to the orders of the day the orders cannot be called for again until the pending business is disposed of.

When the orders of the day are announced, or when they are called for, if it is desired to prolong the discussion of the pending question, some one should move that the time for considering the pending question be extended a certain number of minutes. A two-thirds vote is required for the adoption of this motion as it changes the order of business or program. After the order has been announced and the question is actually pending, it is debatable and may be amended or have any other subsidiary motion applied to it the same as any other main motion. The orders of the day in a mass cannot be laid on the table or postponed, but when an order has been actually taken up it may, by a majority vote, be laid on the table, or postponed, or committed, so that, if there is no other order to interfere, the consideration of the question previously pending will be resumed. Whenever the orders of the day are disposed of, the consideration of the interrupted business is taken up at the point where it was interrupted by the call for the orders of the day. By suspending the rules by a two-thirds vote any question may be taken up out of its proper order.

Orders of the Day. When one or more subjects have been assigned to a particular day or hour (by postponing them to, or making them special orders for, that day or hour, or by adopting a program or order of business), they become the orders of the day for that day or hour, and they cannot be considered before that time, except by a two-thirds vote. They are divided into General Orders and Special Orders, the latter always taking precedence of the former.

A *General Order* is usually made by simply postponing a question to a certain day or hour, or after a certain event. It does not suspend any rule, and therefore cannot interrupt business. But after the appointed hour has arrived it has the preference, when no question is pending, over all other questions except special orders and reconsideration. It cannot be considered before the appointed time except by a reconsideration or by a two-thirds vote. When the order of business provides for orders of the day, questions simply postponed to a meeting, without specifying the hour, come up under that head. If no provision is made for orders of the day, then such postponed questions come up after the disposal of the business pending at the previous adjournment, and after the questions on the calendar that were not disposed of at the previous meeting.

An order of business that specifies the order in which, but not the time when, the business shall be transacted, together with the postponed questions constitutes the general orders. This order cannot be varied from except by general consent or by suspending the rules by a two-thirds vote. If all of this business is not disposed of before adjournment, it becomes "unfinished business," and is treated as unfinished business, as explained in 17 under The Effect Upon Unfinished Business of an Adjournment.

As general orders cannot interrupt the consideration of a pending question, it follows that any general order made for an earlier hour, though made afterwards, by not being disposed of in time may interfere with the general order previously made. Therefore, general orders must take precedence among themselves in the order of the times to which they were postponed, regardless of when the general order was made. If several are appointed for the same time, then they take precedence in the order in which they were made. If several appointed for the same time were made at the same time, then they take precedence in the order in which they were arranged in the motion making the general order.

To *Make a Special Order* requires a two-thirds vote, because it suspends all rules that interfere with its consideration at the specified time, except those relating to motions for adjournment or recess, or to questions of privilege, or to special orders made before it was made. A pending question is made a special order for a future time by "Postponing it and making it a special order for that time." [See Postpone to a Certain Time, **31**, which should be read in connection with this section.] If the question is not pending, the motion to make it a special order for a certain time is a main motion, debatable, amendable, etc. The member desirous of making it a special order should obtain the floor when nothing is pending, and business of that class, or new business, is in order, and say, "I move that the following resolution be made the special order for [specifying the time]," and then reads the resolution and hands it to the chair. Or he may adopt this form: "I offer the following resolution, and move that it be made a special order for the next meeting." Or, in case a committee has been appointed to submit a revision of the constitution, the following resolution may be adopted: "Resolved, That the revision of the constitution be made the special order for Thursday morning and thereafter until it is disposed of." Another way of making special orders is by adopting a program, or order of business, in which is specified the hour for taking up each topic.

Program. It is customary to adopt a program, or order of business, in conventions in session for several days. Since the delegates and invited speakers come from a distance, it is very important that the program be strictly adhered to. No change can be made in it after its adoption by the assembly, except by a two-thirds vote. When the hour assigned to a certain topic arrives, the chair puts to vote any questions pending and announces the topic for the hour. This is done because, under such circumstances, the form of the program implies that the hour, or other time, assigned to each topic is all that can be allowed. But, if any one moves to lay the question on the table, or postpone it to a certain time, or refer it to a committee, the chair should recognize the motion and immediately put it to vote without debate. Should any one move to extend the time allotted the pending question, it should be decided instantly without debate, a two-thirds vote being necessary for the extension. It is seldom that an extension is desirable, as it is unfair to the next topic. When an invited speaker exceeds his time it is extremely discourteous to call for the orders of the day. The chair should have an understanding with invited speakers as to how he will indicate the expiration of their time. This can be done by tapping on a book or a bell. It is usually better to have it understood that the signal will be given one minute before the time expires, or longer if the speaker wishes it, so that he can properly close his address. At the expiration of the time the presiding officer should rise and attract the attention of the speaker and, if he still continues speaking, the chair should say that the time has expired, etc.

A *series of special orders made by a single vote* is treated the same as a program—that is, at the hour assigned to a particular subject it interrupts the question assigned to the previous hour. If it is desired to continue the discussion of the pending topic at another time, it can be laid on the table or postponed until after the close of the interrupting question, by a majority vote.

Special Orders made at different times for specified hours. When special orders that have been made at different times come into conflict, the one that was first made takes precedence of all special orders made afterwards, though the latter were made for an earlier hour. No special order can be made so as to interfere with one previously made. By reconsidering the vote making the first special order, they can be arranged in the order desired. Suppose, after a special order has been made for 3 P. M., one is made for 2 P. M., and still later one is made for 4 P. M.; if the 2 P. M. order is pending at 3 P. M., the order for 3 P. M., having been made first, interrupts it and continues, if not previously disposed of, beyond 4 P. M., regardless of the special order for that hour. When it, the 3 P. M. order, is disposed of, the special order for 2 P. M. is resumed even if it is after 4 o'clock, because the 2 P. M. order was made before the 4 P. M. order. The only exception to this rule is in the case of the hour fixed for recess or adjournment. When that hour arrives the chair announces it and declares the assembly adjourned, or in recess, even though there is a special order pending that was made before the hour for recess or adjournment was fixed. When the chair announces the hour, any one can move to postpone the time for adjournment, or to extend the time for considering the pending question a certain number of minutes. These motions are undebatable, and require a two-thirds vote.

Special Orders when only the day or meeting is specified. Often subjects are made special orders for a meeting without specifying an hour. If the order of business provides for orders of the day, they come up under that head, taking precedence of general orders. If there is no provision for orders of the day, they come up under unfinished business—that is, before new business. If there is no order of business, then they may be called up at any time after the minutes are disposed of.

The Special Order for a Meeting. Sometimes a subject is made *the* special order for a meeting, as for Tuesday morning in a convention, in which case it is announced by the chair as the pending business immediately after the disposal of the minutes. This particular form is used when it is desired to devote an entire meeting, or so much of it as is necessary, to considering a special subject, as the revision of the by-laws. This form of a special order should take precedence of the other forms of special orders. **It is debatable and amendable.**

Art. IV. Incidental Motions.

See 13 for a list and the general characteristics of these motions.

21. Questions of Order and Appeal. A *Question of Order* takes precedence of the pending question out of which it arises; is in order when another has the floor, even interrupting a speech or the reading of a report; does not require a second; cannot be amended or have any other subsidiary motion applied to it; yields to privileged motions and the motion to lay on the table; and must be decided by the presiding officer without debate, unless in doubtful cases he submits the question to the assembly for decision, in which case it is debatable whenever an appeal would be. Before rendering his decision he may request the advice of persons of experience, which advice or opinion should usually be given sitting to avoid the appearance of debate. If the chair is still in doubt, he may submit the question to the assembly for its decision in a manner similar to this: "Mr. A raises the point of order that the amendment just offered [state the amendment] is not germane to the resolution. The chair is in doubt, and submits the question to the assembly. The question is, 'Is the amendment germane to the resolution?'" As no appeal can be taken from the decision of the assembly, this question is open to debate whenever an appeal would be, if the chair decided the question and an appeal were made from that decision. Therefore, it is debatable except when it relates to indecorum, or transgression of the rules of speaking, or to the priority of business, or when it is made during a division of the assembly, or while an undebatable question is pending. The question is put thus: "As many as are of opinion that the amendment is germane [or that the point is well taken] say *aye;* as many as are of a contrary opinion say *no*. The ayes have it, the amendment is in order, and the question is on its adoption." If the negative vote is the larger it would be announced thus: "The noes have it, the amendment is out of order, and the question is on the adoption of the resolution." Whenever the presiding officer decides a question of order, he has the right, without leaving his chair, to state the reasons for his decision, and any two members have the right to appeal from the decision, one making the appeal and the other seconding it.

It is the duty of the presiding officer to enforce the rules and orders of the assembly, without debate or delay. It is also the right of every member who notices the breach of a rule, to insist upon its enforcement. In such a case he rises from his seat and says, "Mr. Chairman, I rise to a point of order." The speaker immediately takes his seat, and the chairman requests the member to state his point of order, which he does and resumes his seat. The chair decides the point, and then, if no appeal is taken and the member has not been guilty of any serious breach of decorum, the chair permits him to resume his speech. But, if his remarks are decided to be improper and any one objects, he cannot continue without a vote of the assembly to that effect. [See 43 for a full treatment of this subject of indecorum in debate]. The question of order must be raised at the time the breach of order occurs, so that after a motion has been discussed it is too late to raise the question as to whether it was in order, or for the chair to rule the motion out of order. The only exception is where the motion is in violation of the laws, or the constitution, by-laws, or standing rules of the organization, or of fundamental parliamentary principles, so that if adopted it would be null and void. In such cases it is never too late to raise a point of order against the motion. This is called raising a question, or point, of order, because the member in effect puts to the chair, whose duty it is to enforce order, the question as to whether there is not now a breach of order.

Instead of the method just described, it is usual, when it is simply a case of improper language used in debate, for the chair to call the speaker to order, or for a member to say, "I call the gentleman to order." The chairman decides whether the speaker is in or out of order, and proceeds as before.

Appeal. An appeal may be made from any decision of the chair (except when another appeal is pending), but it can be made only at the time the ruling is made. It is in order while another member has the floor. If any debate or business has intervened it is too late to appeal. An answer to a parliamentary inquiry is not a decision, and therefore cannot be appealed from. While an appeal is pending a question of order may be raised, which the chair decides peremptorily, there being no appeal from this decision. But the question as to the correctness of the ruling can be brought up afterwards when no other business is pending. An appeal yields to privileged motions, and to the motion to lay on the table. The effect of subsidiary motions is as follows: An appeal cannot be amended. If the decision from which an appeal is taken is of such a nature that the reversal of the ruling would not in any way affect the consideration of, or action on, the main question, then the main question does not adhere to the appeal, and its consideration is resumed as soon as the appeal is laid on the table, postponed, etc. But if the ruling affects the consideration of, or action on, the main question, then the main question adheres to the appeal, and when the latter is laid on the table, or postponed, the main question goes with it. Thus, if the appeal is from the decision that a proposed amendment is out of order and the appeal is laid on the table, it would be absurd to come to final action on the main question and then afterwards reverse the decision of the chair and take up the amendment when there was no question to amend. The vote on an appeal may be reconsidered.

An appeal cannot be debated when it relates simply to indecorum, or to transgression of the rules of speaking, or to the priority of business, or if made during a division of the assembly, or while the immediately pending question is undebatable. When debatable, as it is in all other cases, no member is allowed to speak more than once except the presiding officer, who may at the close of the debate answer the arguments against the decision. Whether debatable or not, the chairman when stating the question on the appeal may, without leaving the chair, state the reasons for his decision.

When a member wishes to appeal from the decision of the chair he rises as soon as the decision is made, even though another has the floor, and without waiting to be recognized by the chair, says, "Mr. Chairman, I appeal from the decision of the chair." If this appeal is seconded, the chair should state clearly the question at issue, and his reasons for the decision if he thinks it necessary, and then state the question thus: "The question is, 'Shall the decision of the chair stand as the judgment of the assembly [or society, or club, etc.] ?' " or, "Shall the decision of the chair be sustained?" To put the question he would say, "Those in the affirmative say *aye*," and after the affirmative vote has been taken he would say, "Those in the negative say *no*. The ayes have it and the decision of the chair is sustained [or stands as the judgment of the assembly]." Or, "The noes have it and the decision of the chair is reversed." In either case he immediately announces what is before the assembly as the result of the vote. If there is a tie vote the chair is sustained, and if the chair is a member of the assembly he may vote to make it a tie, on the principle that the decision of the chair stands until reversed by a majority, including the chairman if he is a member of the assembly. In stating the question, the word "assembly" should be replaced by "society," or "club," or "board," etc., as the case may be. The announcement of a vote is not a decision of the chair. If a member doubts the correctness of the announcement he cannot appeal, but should call for a "Division" [25].

22. Suspension of the Rules.* The mo-

* In Congress the former practice was to suspend the rule as to the order of business in order to consider a particular bill, but now it is customary "to suspend the rule and pass" the resolution or bill. H. R. Rule 27 contains the following:

"1. No rule shall be suspended except by a vote of two-thirds of the members voting, a quorum being present; nor shall the Speaker entertain a motion to suspend the

tion to suspend the rules may be made at any time when no question is pending; or while a question is pending, provided it is for a purpose connected with that question. It yields to all the privileged motions (except a call for the orders of the day), to the motion to lay on the table, and to incidental motions arising out of itself. It is undebatable and cannot be amended or have any other subsidiary motion applied to it, nor can a vote on it be reconsidered, nor can a motion to suspend the rules for the same purpose be renewed at the same meeting except by unanimous consent, though it may be renewed after an adjournment, even if the next meeting is held the same day.

When the assembly wishes to do something that cannot be done without violating its own rules, and yet it is not in conflict with its constitution, or by-laws, or with the fundamental principles of parliamentary law, it "suspends the rules that interfere with" the proposed action. The object of the suspension

---

rules except on the first and third Mondays of each month, preference being given on the first Monday to individuals and on the third Monday to committees, and during the last six days of a session.

"2. All motions to suspend the rules shall, before being submitted to the House, be seconded by a majority by tellers, if demanded.

"3. When a motion to suspend the rules has been seconded, it shall be in order, before the final vote is taken thereon, to debate the proposition to be voted upon for forty minutes, one-half of such time to be given to debate in favor of, and one-half to debate in opposition to, such proposition; and the same right of debate shall be allowed whenever the previous question has been ordered on any proposition on which there has been no debate."

must be specified, and nothing else can be done under the suspension. The rules that can be suspended are those relating to priority of business, or to business procedure, or to admission to the meetings, etc., and would usually be comprised under the heads of rules of order. Sometimes societies include in their by-laws some rules relating to the transaction of business without any intention, evidently, of giving these rules any greater stability than is possessed by other rules of their class, and they may be suspended the same as if they were called rules of order. A standing rule as defined in 67 may be suspended by a majority vote. But sometimes the term "standing rules" is applied to what are strictly rules of order, and then, like rules of order, they require a two-thirds vote for their suspension. Nothing that requires previous notice and a two-thirds vote for its amendment can be suspended by less than a two-thirds vote.

No rule can be suspended when the negative vote is as large as the minority protected by that rule; nor can a rule protecting absentees be suspended even by general consent or a unanimous vote. For instance, a rule requiring notice of a motion to be given at a previous meeting cannot be suspended by a unanimous vote, as it protects absentees who do not give their consent. A rule requiring officers to be elected by ballot cannot be suspended by a unanimous vote, because the rule protects a minority of one from exposing his vote, and this he must do if he votes openly in the negative, or objects to giving general consent. Nor can this result be accomplished by voting that the ballot of the assembly be cast by the secretary or any one else, as this does away with the essential principle of the ballot, namely, secrecy, and is a suspension of the by-law, and practically allows a viva voce vote. If it is desired to allow the suspension of a by-law that cannot be suspended under these rules, then it is necessary to provide in the by-laws for its suspension.

The *Form* of this motion is, "to suspend the rules that interfere with," etc., stating the object of the suspension, as, "the consideration of a resolution on ....," which resolution is immediately offered after the rules are suspended, the chair recognizing for that purpose the member that moved to suspend the rules. Or, if it is desired to consider a question which has been laid on the table, and cannot be taken up at that time because that class of business is not then in order, or to consider a question that has been postponed to another time, or that is in the order of business for another time, then the motion may be made thus, "I move to suspend the rules and take up [or consider] the resolution ...." When the object is not to take up a question for discussion but to adopt it without debate, the motion is made thus: "I move to suspend the rules and adopt [or agree to] the following resolution," which is then read: or, "I move to suspend the rules, and adopt [or agree to] the resolution on ...." The same form may be used in a case like this: "I move to suspend the rules, and admit to the privileges of the floor members of sister societies," which merely admits them to the hall.

Instead of a formal motion to suspend the rules, it is more usual to ask for general consent to do the particular business that is out of order. As soon as the request is made the chair inquires if there is any objection, and if no one objects, he directs the member to proceed just as if the rules had been suspended by a formal vote. [See General Consent **48.**]

23. Objection to the Consideration of a Question. An objection may be made to the consideration of any original main motion, and to no others, provided it is made before there is any debate or before any subsidiary motion is stated. Thus, it may be applied to petitions and to communications that are not from a superior body, as well as to resolutions. It cannot be applied to incidental main motions [**11**], such as amendments to by-laws, or to reports of committees on subjects referred to them, etc. It is similar to a question of order in that it can be made when another has the floor, and does not require a second; and as the chairman can call a member to order, so he can put this question, if he deems it advisable, upon his own responsibility. It cannot be debated, or amended, or have any other subsidiary motion applied to it. It yields to privileged motions and to the motion to lay on the table. A negative, but not an affirmative vote on the consideration may be reconsidered.*

When an original main motion is made and any member wishes to prevent its consideration, he rises, although another has the floor, and says, "Mr. Chairman, I object to its consideration." The chairman immediately puts the question, "The consideration of the question has been objected to: Will the assembly consider it? [or, Shall the question be considered?]" If decided in the negative by a two-thirds vote, the whole matter is dismissed for that session; otherwise, the discussion continues as if this objection had never been made. The same question may be introduced at any succeeding session.

The *Object* of this motion is not to cut off debate (for which other motions are provided)

* In Congress the introduction of a question may be prevented temporarily by a majority vote under H. R. Rule 16, §3, which is as follows: "3. When any motion or proposition is made, the question, Will the House now consider it? shall not be put unless demanded by a member." If the House refuses to consider a bill the vote cannot be reconsidered. But this refusal does not prevent the question's being again introduced the same session. In assemblies having brief sessions lasting usually only a few hours, or at most not over a week, it is necessary that the assembly have the power by a two-thirds vote to decide that a question shall not be introduced during that session. As the refusal to consider the question prevents its renewal during the session, the vote may be reconsidered.

but to enable the assembly to avoid altogether any question which it may deem irrelevant, unprofitable, or contentious. If the chair considers the question entirely outside the objects of the society, he should rule it out of order, from which decision an appeal may be taken.

Objection to the consideration of a question must not be confounded with objecting where unanimous consent, or a majority vote, is required. Thus, in case of the minority of a committee desiring to submit their views, a single member saying, "I object," prevents it, unless the assembly by a majority vote grants them permission.

24. Division of a Question, and Consideration by Paragraph. *Division of a Question.** The motion to divide a question can be applied only to main motions and to amendments. It takes precedence of nothing but the motion to postpone indefinitely, and yields to all privileged, incidental, and subsidiary motions except to amend and to postpone indefinitely. It may be amended but can have no other subsidiary motion applied to it. It is undebatable. It may be made at any time when the question to be divided, or the motion to postpone indefinitely, is immediately pending, even after the previous question has been

* Section 6 of H. R. Rule 16 is as follows: "6. On the demand of any member, before the question is put, a question shall be divided if it include propositions so distinct in substance that one being taken away a substantive proposition shall remain."

ordered. But it is preferable to divide the question when it is first introduced. When divided each resolution or proposition is considered and voted on separately, the same as if it had been offered alone. The motion to adopt, which was pending when the question was divided, applies to all the parts into which the question has been divided and should not, therefore, be repeated. The formality of a vote on dividing the question is generally dispensed with, as it is usually arranged by general consent. But if this cannot be done, then a formal motion to divide is necessary, specifying the exact method of division.

When a motion relating to a certain subject contains several parts, each of which is capable of standing as a complete proposition if the others are removed, it can be divided into two or more propositions to be considered and voted on as distinct questions, by the assembly's adopting a motion to divide the question in a specified manner. The motion must clearly state how the question is to be divided, and any one else may propose a different division, and these different propositions, or amendments, should be treated as filling blanks; that is, they should be voted on in the order in which they are made, unless they suggest different numbers of questions, when the largest number is voted on first. If a resolution includes several distinct propositions, but is so written that they cannot be separated without its being rewritten, the question cannot be divided. The division must not require the secretary to do more than to mechanically separate the resolution into the required parts, prefixing to each part the words "*Resolved*, That," or "*Ordered*, That," and dropping conjunctions when necessary, and replacing pronouns by the nouns for which they stand, wherever the division makes it necessary. When the question is divided, each separate question must be a proper one for the assembly to act upon, if none of the others is adopted. Thus, a motion to "commit with instructions" is indivisible; because, if divided, and the motion to commit should fail, then the other motion, to instruct the committee, would be absurd, as there would be no committee to instruct. The motion to "strike out certain words and insert others" is strictly one proposition and therefore indivisible.

If a series of independent resolutions relating to different subjects is included in one motion, it must be divided on the request of a single member, which request may be made while another has the floor. But however complicated a single proposition may be, no member has a right to insist upon its division. His remedy is to move that it be divided, if it is capable of division, or, if not, to move to strike out the objectionable parts. A motion to strike out a name in a resolution brings the assembly to a vote on that name just as well as would a division of the question, if it were allowed to go to that extent, which it is not. If a series of resolutions is proposed as a substitute for another series, such a motion is incapable of division; but a motion can be made to strike out any of the resolutions before the vote is taken on the substitution. After they have been substituted it is too late to strike out any of them. When a committee reports a number of amendments to a resolution referred to it, one vote may be taken on adopting, or agreeing to, all the amendments provided no one objects. But if a single member requests separate votes on one or more of the amendments, they must be considered separately. The others may all be voted on together.

Consideration by Paragraph or Seriatim. Where an elaborate proposition is submitted, like a series of resolutions on one subject, or a set of by-laws, the parts being intimately connected, it should not be divided. The division would add greatly to the difficulty of perfecting the different paragraphs or by-laws by amendments. If the paragraphs are adopted separately, and amendments to succeeding paragraphs make it necessary to amend a preceding one, it can be done only by first reconsidering the vote on the preceding paragraph. In the case of by-laws the trouble is increased, because each by-law goes into effect as soon as adopted, and its amendment is controlled by any by-law or rule that may have been adopted on the subject. When the paragraphs are voted on separately no vote should be taken on the whole. But in all such cases the proper course is to consider the proposition by paragraph, or section, or resolution, or, as it is often called, *seriatim*. The chair should always adopt this course when the question consists of several paragraphs or resolutions, unless he thinks the assembly wishes to act on them immediately as a whole, when he asks if they shall be taken up by paragraph, and the matter is settled informally. Should the chair neglect to take up the proposition by paragraph, any one may move that the proposition be considered by paragraph, or seriatim.

The method of procedure in acting upon a complicated report, as, a set of by-laws, or a series of resolutions that cannot well be divided, is as follows, the word "paragraph" being used to designate the natural subdivisions, whether they are paragraphs, sections, articles, or resolutions. The member submitting the report, having obtained the floor, says that such and such a committee submits the following report; or, that the committee recommends the adoption of the following resolutions. In either case he reads the report, or resolutions, and moves their adoption. Should he neglect to move their adoption, the chair should call for such a motion, or he may assume the motion and state the question accordingly. The chairman, or the secretary, or the member who reported it, as the chair decides is for the best interest of the assembly, then reads the first paragraph, which is explained by the reporting member, after which the chair asks, "Are there any amendments to this paragraph?" The paragraph is then open to debate and amendment. When no further amendments are proposed to this paragraph, the chair says, "There being no further amendments to this paragraph the next will be read." In a similar manner each paragraph in succession is read, explained if necessary, debated, and amended, the paragraphs being amended but not adopted. After all the paragraphs have been amended, the chair says the entire by-law, or paper, or resolution is open to amendment, when additional paragraphs may be inserted and any paragraph may be further amended. When the paper is satisfactorily amended, the preamble, if any, is treated the same way, and then a single vote is taken on the adoption of the entire paper, report, or series of resolutions. If the previous question is ordered on a resolution, or series of resolutions, or on a set of by-laws, before the preamble has been considered it does not apply to the preamble, unless expressly so stated, because the preamble cannot be considered until after debate has ceased on the resolutions or by-laws. It is not necessary to amend the numbers of the sections, paragraphs, etc., as it is the duty of the secretary to make all such corrections where changes are rendered necessary by amendments.

25. Division of the Assembly, and other Motions relating to Voting. *A Division of the Assembly** may be called for, without obtaining the floor, at any time after the question has been put, even after the vote has been announced and another has the floor, provided the vote was taken viva voce, or by show of hands, and it is called for before another motion has been made. This call, or motion, is made by saying, "I call for a division," or "I doubt the vote," or simply by calling out, "Division." It does not require a second, and cannot be debated, or amended, or have any other subsidiary motion applied to it. As soon as a division is called for, the chair proceeds again to take the vote, this time by having the affirmative rise, and then when they are seated having the negative rise. While any member has the right to insist upon a rising vote, or a division, where there is any question as to the vote being a true expression of the will of the assembly, the chair should not permit this privilege to be abused to the annoyance of the assembly, by members constantly demanding a division where there is a full vote and no question as to which side is in the majority. It requires a majority vote to order the vote to be counted, or to be taken by yeas and nays

* See foot note, page 40, for the rule of Congress.

(roll call) or by ballot. These motions are incidental to the question that is pending or has just been pending, and cannot be debated. When different methods are suggested they are usually treated not as amendments, but like filling blanks, the vote being taken first on the one taking the most time. In practice the method of taking a vote is generally agreed upon without the formality of a vote.

When the vote is taken by ballot during a meeting of the assembly, as soon as the chair thinks all have voted who wish to, he inquires if all have voted, and if there is no response he declares the polls closed, and the tellers proceed to count the vote. If a formal motion is made to close the polls it should not be recognized until all have presumably voted, and then it requires a two-thirds vote like motions to close debate or nominations. If members enter afterwards and it is desired to reopen the polls it can be done by a majority vote. None of these motions are debatable.

26. Motions relating to Nominations. If no method of making nominations is designated by the by-laws or rules, and the assembly has adopted no order on the subject, any one can make a motion prescribing the method of nomination for an office to be filled. If the election is pending, this motion is incidental to it; if the election is not pending, it is an incidental main motion. It is undebatable and when it is an incidental motion it can have no subsidiary motion applied to it except to amend. It yields to privileged motions. The motion may provide for nominations being made by the chair; or from the floor, or open nominations as it is also called; or for a nominating committee to be appointed; or for nominations to be made by ballot; or by mail. [See Nominations and Elections, **66**.]

Closing and Reopening Nominations. Before proceeding to an election, if nominations have been made from the floor or by a committee, the chair should inquire if there are any further nominations. If there is no response he declares the nominations closed. In very large bodies it is customary to make a motion to close nominations, but until a reasonable time has been given, this motion is not in order. It is a main motion, incidental to the nominations and elections, cannot be debated, can be amended as to the time, but can have no other subsidiary motion applied to it. It yields to privileged motions, and requires a two-thirds vote as it deprives members of one of their rights.

If for any reason it is desired to reopen nominations it may be done by a majority vote. This motion is undebatable. It can be amended as to the time, but no other subsidiary motion can be applied to it. It yields to privileged motions.

27. Requests Growing out of the Business of the Assembly. During the meetings of a deliberative assembly there are occasions when members wish to obtain information, or to do or to have done things that necessitate their making a request. Among these are the following, which will be treated separately:

(*a*) *Parliamentary Inquiry;*
(*b*) *Request for Information;*
(*c*) *Leave to Withdraw a Motion;*
(*d*) *Reading Papers;*
(*e*) *To be Excused from a Duty;*
(*f*) *For any other Privilege.*

(*a*) *Parliamentary Inquiry.* A parliamentary inquiry, if it relates to a question that requires immediate attention, may be made while another has the floor, or may even interrupt a speech. It should not, however, be permitted to interrupt a speaker any more than is necessary to do justice to the inquirer. It yields to privileged motions, if they were in order when the inquiry was made, and it cannot be debated or amended or have any other subsidiary motion applied to it. The inquirer does not obtain the floor, but rises and says, "Mr. Chairman, I rise to a parliamentary inquiry." The chairman asks him to state his inquiry, and if he deems it pertinent, he answers it. Or, if the inquiry is made when another has the floor, and there is no necessity for answering it until the speech is finished, the chair may defer his answer until the speaker has closed his remarks. While it is not the duty of the chairman to answer questions of parliamentary law in general, it is his duty when requested by a member, to answer any questions on parliamentary law pertinent to the pending business that may be necessary to enable the member to make a suitable motion or to raise a point of order. The chairman is supposed to be familiar with parliamentary law, while many of the members are not. A member wishing to raise a point of order and yet in doubt, should rise to a parliamentary inquiry and ask for information. Or, for instance, he may wish to have the assembly act immediately on a subject that is in the hands of a committee, and he does not know how to accomplish it;—his recourse is a parliamentary inquiry.

(*b*) *Request for Information.* A request for information relating to the pending business is treated just as a parliamentary inquiry, and has the same privileges. The inquirer rises and says, "Mr. Chairman, I rise for information," or, "I rise to a point of information," whereupon the chair directs him to state the point upon which he desires information, and the procedure continues as in case of a parliamentary inquiry. If the information is desired of the speaker, instead of the chair, the inquirer upon rising says, "Mr. Chairman, I should like to ask the gentleman a question." The chairman inquires if the speaker is willing to be interrupted, and if he consents, he directs the inquirer to proceed. The inquirer then asks the question through the chair, thus, "Mr. Chairman, I should like to ask the gentleman," etc. The reply is made in the same way, as it is not in order for members to address one another in the assembly. While each speaker addresses the chair, the chair remains silent during the conversation. If the speaker consents to the interruption the time consumed is taken out of his time.

(*c*) *Leave to Withdraw or Modify a Motion.** A request for leave to withdraw a motion, or a motion to grant such leave, may be made at any time before voting on the question has commenced, even though the motion has been amended. It requires no second. It may be made while incidental or subsidiary motions are pending, and these motions cease to be before the assembly when the question to which they are incidental or subsidiary is withdrawn. It yields to privileged motions, and cannot be amended or have any other subsidiary motion applied to it. It is undebatable. When it is too late to renew it, the motion to reconsider cannot be withdrawn without unanimous consent. When a motion is withdrawn, the effect is the same as if it had never been made. Until a motion is stated by the chairman, the mover may withdraw or modify it

* In Congress a motion "may be withdrawn at any time before a decision or amendment." H. R. Rule 16, §2. The rule given above, which is in accordance with the common parliamentary law, is better adapted to ordinary assemblies.

without asking consent of any one. If he modifies it the seconder may withdraw his second. After the question has been stated it is in possession of the assembly, and he can neither withdraw nor modify it without the consent of the assembly. When the mover requests permission to modify or withdraw his motion, the chair asks if there is any objection, and if there is none he announces that the motion is withdrawn or modified in such and such a way, as the case may be. If any one objects the chair puts the question on granting the request, or a motion may be made to grant it. In case the mover of a main motion wishes to accept an amendment that has been offered, without obtaining the floor, he says, "Mr. Chairman, I accept the amendment." If no objection is made the chair announces the question as amended. If any one objects, the chair states the question on the amendment, as it can be accepted only by general consent. A request for leave to do anything is treated the same as a motion to grant the leave except that the request must be made by the maker of the motion it is proposed to modify, while the motion to grant the leave is made by some one else and therefore requires no second as it is favored by the one making the request.

(*d*) *Reading Papers.* If any member objects, a member has no right to read, or have the clerk read, from any paper or book, as a part of his speech, without the permission of the assembly. The request or the motion to grant such permission yields to privileged motions. It cannot be debated, or amended, or have any other subsidiary motion applied to it. It is customary, however, to allow members to read printed extracts as parts of their speeches, as long as they do not abuse the privilege.

Where papers are laid before the assembly, every member has a right to have them read once, or if there is debate or amendment he has the right to have them read again, before he can be compelled to vote on them. Whenever a member asks for the reading of any such paper evidently for information, and not for delay, the chair should direct it to be read, if no one objects. But a member has not the right to have anything read (excepting as stated above) without permission of the assembly. If a member was absent from the hall when the paper under consideration was read, even though absent on duty, he cannot insist on its being again read, as the convenience of the assembly is of more importance than that of a single member.

(*e*) *To be Excused from a Duty.* If a member is elected to office, or appointed on a committee, or has any other duty placed on him, and he is unable or unwilling to perform the duty, if present he should decline it immediately, and if absent he should, upon learning of the fact, at once notify the secretary or president orally or in writing that he cannot accept the duty. In most organizations members cannot be compelled to accept office or perform any duties not required by the by-laws, and therefore they have the right to decline office. But if a member does not immediately decline, by his silence he accepts the office, and is under obligation to perform the duty until there has been a reasonable opportunity for his resignation to be accepted. The secretary, for instance, cannot relieve himself from the responsibility of his office by resigning. His responsibility as secretary does not cease until his resignation is accepted, or, at least, until there has been a reasonable time for its acceptance. It is seldom good policy to decline to accept a resignation. As a member has no right to continue to hold an office the duties of which he cannot or will not perform, so a society has no right to force an office on an unwilling member. When a member declines an office, no motion is necessary, unless the by-laws of the society make the performance of such duties obligatory upon members. If the member is present at the election, the vacancy is filled as if no one had been elected. If the member was not present at the election, when the chair announces his refusal to take the office, as it is a question of privilege relating to the organization of the society, the election to fill the vacancy may take place at once unless notice is required, or other provision for filling vacancies is provided by the by-laws. In the case of a resignation, the chair may at once state the question on accepting it, or a motion to that effect may be made. In either case it is debatable and may have any subsidiary motion applied to it. It yields to privileged and incidental motions.

(*f*) *Request for Any Other Privilege.* When any request is to be made the member rises and addresses the chair, and as soon as he catches the eye of the chairman, states at once why he rises. He should rise as soon as a member yields the floor, and, though the floor is assigned to another, he still makes his request. He should never interrupt a member while speaking unless he is sure that the urgency of the case justifies it. As a rule all such questions are settled by general consent, or informally, but, if objection is made, a vote is taken. An explanation may be requested or given, but there is no debate. As these requests arise, they should be treated so as to interrupt the proceedings as little as is consistent with the demands of justice.

Art. V. Subsidiary Motions.

See **12** for a list and the general characteristics of these motions.

28. To Lay on the Table. This motion takes precedence of all other subsidiary [12] motions and of such incidental [13] questions as are pending at the time it is made. It yields to privileged [14] motions and such motions as are incidental to itself. It is undebatable and cannot have any subsidiary motion applied to it. It may be applied to any main [11] motion; to any question of privilege or order of the day, after it is before the assembly for consideration; to an appeal that does not adhere to the main question, so that the action on the latter would not be affected by the reversal of the chair's decision; or to the motion to reconsider when immediately pending, in which case the question to be reconsidered goes to the table also. No motion that has another motion adhering to it can be laid on the table by itself; if laid on the table it carries with it everything that adheres to it. When a motion is taken from the table [35] everything is in the same condition, as far as practicable, as when the motion was laid on the table, except that if not taken up until the next session the effect of the previous question is exhausted. If debate has been closed by ordering the previous question, or otherwise, up to the moment of taking the last vote under the order, the questions still before the assembly may be laid on the table. Thus, if, while a resolution and an amendment and a motion to commit are pending, the previous question is ordered on the series of questions, and the vote has been taken and lost on the motion to commit, it is in order to lay on the table the resolution, which carries with it the adhering amendment.

This motion cannot be applied to anything except a question actually pending, therefore it is not in order to lay on the table a class of questions, as the orders of the day, or unfinished business, or reports of committees, because they are not pending questions, as only one main motion can be pending at a time.

To accomplish the desired object, which is evidently to reach a special subject or class of business, the proper course is to suspend the rules by a two-thirds vote and take up the desired question or class of business. Sometimes when it is desired to pass over the next order or class of business, that business is "passed," as it is called, by general consent. In such case, as soon as the business for which it was "passed" is disposed of, it is then taken up. By general consent, the business to come before the assembly may be considered in any order the assembly desires.

If a motion to lay on the table has been made and lost, or if a question laid on the table has been taken from the table, it shows that the assembly wishes to consider the question now, and therefore a motion made the same day to lay that question on the table is out of order until there has been material progress in business or debate, or unless an unforeseen urgent matter requires immediate attention. The assembly cannot be required to vote again the same day on laying the question on the table unless there is such a change in the state of affairs as to make it a new question. Motions relating to adjournment or recess, made and lost, are not business justifying the renewal of the motion to lay on the table, but the renewal of the motion might be justified after a vote on an important amendment, or on the motion to commit. A vote on laying on the table cannot be reconsidered, because, if lost the motion may be renewed as soon as there has been material progress in debate or business, or even before if anything unforeseen occurs of such an urgent nature as to require immediate attention; and if adopted the question may be taken from the table as soon as the interrupting business has been disposed of and while no question is pending, and business of this class, or new or unfinished business, is in order.

The *Form* of this motion is, "I move to lay the question on the table," or, "That the question be laid on the table," or, "That the question lie on the table." It cannot be qualified in any way; if it is qualified, thus, "To lay the question on the table until 2 P. M.," the chair should state it properly as a motion to postpone until 2 P. M., which is a debatable question, and not the motion to lay on the table.

The *Object** of this motion is to enable the

---

* The common parliamentary law in regard to this motion is thus laid down in Section 33 of Jefferson's Manual, the authority in both Houses of Congress: "4. When the House has something else which claims its present attention, but would be willing to reserve in their power to take up a proposition whenever it shall suit them, they

assembly, in order to attend to more urgent business, to lay aside the pending question in such a way that its consideration may be resumed at the will of the assembly as easily as if it were a new question, and in preference to new questions competing with it for consideration. It is to the interest of the assembly that this object should be attained instantly by a majority vote, and therefore this motion must either apply to, or take precedence of, every debatable motion whatever its rank. It is undebatable, and requires only a majority vote, notwithstanding the fact that if not taken from the table the question is suppressed. These are dangerous privileges which are given to no other motion whose adoption would result in final action on a main motion. There is a great temptation to make an improper use of them, and lay questions on the table for the

---

order it to lie on their table. It may then be called for at any time." But, on account of the enormous number of bills introduced each session and the possibility of considering only a small fraction of them, Congress has been obliged to find some way by which the majority can quickly kill a bill. The high rank and undebatability of this motion enabled it to be used for this purpose by simply allowing its mover the right of recognition in preference to the member reporting the bill, and then not allowing a question to be taken from the table except under a suspension of the rules (unless it is a privileged matter), which requires a two-thirds vote. This complete revolution in the use of the motion to lay on the table renders all the practice of Congress in regard to this motion useless for any ordinary deliberative assembly. It is the extreme of a "gag law," and is only justifiable in an assembly where it is impossible to attend to one-tenth of the bills and resolutions introduced. In Congress, to lay on the table and the previous question require the same vote (a majority), and in all ordinary societies where to lay on the table is habitually used to kill questions, it should require the same vote as the previous question, namely, two-thirds.

purpose of instantly suppressing them by a majority vote, instead of using the previous question, the legitimate motion to bring the assembly to an immediate vote. The fundamental principles of parliamentary law require a two-thirds vote for every motion that suppresses a main question for the session without free debate. The motion to lay on the table being undebatable, and requiring only a majority vote, and having the highest rank of all subsidiary motions, is in direct conflict with these principles, if used to suppress a question. If habitually used in this way, it should, like the other motions to suppress without debate, require a two-thirds vote.

The minority has no remedy for the unfair use of this motion, but the evil can be slightly diminished as follows: The person who introduces a resolution is sometimes cut off from speaking by the motion to lay the question on the table being made as soon as the chair states the question, or even before. In such cases the introducer of the resolution should always claim the floor, to which he is entitled, and make his speech. Persons are commonly in such a hurry to make this motion that they neglect to address the chair and thus obtain the floor. In such case one of the minority should address the chair quickly, and if not given the floor, make the point of order that he is the first one to address the chair, and that the other member, not having the floor, was not entitled to make a motion [**3**].

As motions laid on the table are merely temporarily laid aside, the majority should remember that the minority may all stay to the moment of final adjournment and then be in the majority, and take up and pass the resolutions laid on the table. They may also take the question from the table at the next meeting in societies having regular meetings as frequently as quarterly. The safer and fairer method is to object to the consideration of the question if it is so objectionable that it is not desired to allow even its introducer to speak on it; or, if there has been debate so it cannot be objected to, then to move the previous question, which, if adopted, immediately brings the assembly to a vote. These are legitimate motions for getting at the sense of the members at once as to whether they wish the subject discussed, and, as they require a two-thirds vote, no one has a right to object to their being adopted.

The *Effect* of the adoption of this motion is to place on the table, that is, in charge of the secretary, the pending question and everything adhering to it; so, if an amendment is pending to a motion to refer a resolution to a committee, and the question is laid on the table, all these questions go together to the table, and when taken from the table they all come up together. An amendment proposed to anything already adopted is a main motion, and therefore when laid on the table, does not carry with it the thing proposed to be amended. A question of privilege may be laid on the table without carrying with it the question it interrupted. In legislative bodies, and all others that do not have regular sessions as often as quarterly, questions laid on the table remain there for that entire session, unless taken up before the session closes. In deliberative bodies with regular sessions as frequent as quarterly, the sessions usually are very short and questions laid on the table remain there until the close of the next regular session, if not taken up earlier; just as in the same assemblies a question can be postponed to the next session, and the effect of the motion to reconsider, if not called up, does not terminate until the close of the next session. The reasons for any one of these rules apply with nearly equal force to the others. While a question is on the table no motion on the same subject is in order that would in any way affect the question that is on the table; it is necessary first to take the question from the table and move the new one as a substitute, or to make such other motion as is adapted to the case.

29. The Previous Question* takes prece-

---

* The previous question is the only motion used in the House of Representatives for closing debate. It may be ordered by a majority vote. If there has been no previous debate on the subject, forty minutes of debate, to be equally divided between those opposed to and those in favor of the proposition, is allowed after the previous question has been ordered. The motion is not allowed in the Senate. House Rule 17 is as follows:

"1. There shall be a motion for the previous question, which, being ordered by a majority of members voting, if a quorum be present, shall have the effect to cut off all debate and bring the House to a direct vote upon the immediate question or questions on which it has been asked and ordered. The previous question may be asked and ordered upon a single motion, a series of motions allowable under the rules, or an amendment or amendments, or may be made to embrace all authorized motions or amendments and include the bill to its passage or rejection. It shall be in order, pending the motion for, or after the previous question shall have been ordered on its passage, for the Speaker to entertain and submit a motion to commit, with or without instructions, to a standing or select committee.

"2. A call of the House shall not be in order after the previous question is ordered, unless it shall appear upon an actual count by the Speaker that a quorum is not present.

"3. All incidental questions of order arising after a motion is made for the previous question, and pending such motion, shall be decided, whether on appeal or otherwise, without debate."

dence of all subsidiary [12] motions except to lay on the table, and yields to privileged [14] and incidental [13] motions, and to the motion to lay on the table. It is undebatable, and cannot be amended or have any other subsidiary motion applied to it. The effect of an amendment may be obtained by calling for, or moving, the previous question on a different set of the pending questions (which must be consecutive and include the immediately pending question), in which case the vote is taken first on the motion which orders the previous question on the largest number of questions. It may be applied to any debatable or amendable motion or motions, and if unqualified it applies only to the immediately pending motion. It may be qualified so as to apply to a series of pending questions, or to a consecutive part of a series beginning with the immediately pending question. It requires a two-thirds vote for its adoption. After the previous question has been ordered, up to the time of taking the last vote under it, the questions that have not been voted on may be laid on the table, but can have no other subsidiary motions applied to them. An appeal made after the previous question has been demanded or ordered and before its exhaustion, is undebatable. The previous question, before any vote has been taken under it, may be reconsidered, but not after its partial execution. As no one would vote to reconsider the vote ordering the previous question who was not opposed to the previous question, it follows that if the motion to reconsider prevails, it will be impossible to secure a two-thirds vote for the previous question, and, therefore, if it is voted to reconsider the previous question it is considered as rejecting that question and placing the business as it was before the previous question was moved. If a vote taken under the previous question is reconsidered before the previous question is exhausted, there can be no debate or amendment of the proposition; but if the reconsideration is after the previous question is exhausted, then the motion to reconsider, as well as the question to be reconsidered, is divested of the previous question and is debatable. If lost, the previous question may be renewed after sufficient progress in debate to make it a new question.

The *Form* of this motion is, "I move [or demand, or call for] the previous question on [here specify the motions on which it is desired to be ordered]." As it cannot be debated or amended, it must be voted on immediately. The form of putting the question* is, "The previous question is moved [or demanded, or called for] on [specify the motions on which the previous question is demanded].

---

* The Congressional form of putting this question is, "The gentleman from............demands the previous question. As many as are in favor of ordering the previous question will say *Aye;* as many as are opposed will say *No.*"

As many as are in favor of ordering the previous question on [repeat the motions] will rise." When they are seated he continues, "Those opposed will rise. There being two-thirds in favor of the motion, the affirmative has it and the previous question is ordered on [repeat the motions upon which it is ordered]. The question is [or recurs] on [state the immediately pending question]. As many as are in favor," etc. If the previous question is ordered the chair immediately proceeds to put to vote the questions on which it was ordered until all the votes are taken, or there is an affirmative vote on postponing definitely or indefinitely, or committing, either of which exhausts the previous question. If there can be the slightest doubt as to the vote the chair should take it again immediately, counting each side. If less than two-thirds vote in the affirmative, the chair announces the vote thus: "There not being two-thirds in favor of the motion, the negative has it and the motion is lost. The question is on," etc., the chair stating the question on the immediately pending question, which is again open to debate and amendment, the same as if the previous question had not been demanded.

The question may be put in a form similar to this: "The previous question has been moved on the motion to commit and its amendment. As many as are in favor of now putting the question on the motion to commit and its amendment will rise; those opposed will rise. There being two-thirds in favor of the motion, the debate is closed on the motion to commit and its amendment, and the question is on the amendment," etc. While this form is allowable, yet it is better to conform to the regular parliamentary form as given above.

The *Object* of the previous question is to bring the assembly at once to a vote on the immediately pending question and on such other pending questions as may be specified in the demand. It is the proper motion to use for this purpose, whether the object is to adopt or to kill the proposition on which it is ordered, without further debate or motions to amend.

The *Effect** of ordering the previous question is to close debate immediately, to prevent the moving of amendments or any other subsidiary motions except to lay on the table, and to bring the assembly at once to a vote on the immediately pending question, and such other pending questions as were specified in the demand, or motion. If the previous question is ordered on more than one question, then its effect extends to those questions and is not exhausted until they are voted on, or they are disposed of as shown below under exhaustion

---

* The former practice of allowing the member reporting a bill from a committee to close the debate with a speech after the previous question has been ordered, has been abandoned by Congress.

of the previous question. If the previous question is voted down, the discussion continues as if this motion had not been made. The effect of the previous question does not extend beyond the session in which it was adopted. Should any of the questions upon which it was ordered come before the assembly at a future session they are divested of the previous question and are open to debate and amendment.

The previous question is *Exhausted* during the session as follows:

(1) When the previous question is unqualified, its effect terminates as soon as the vote is taken on the immediately pending question.

(2) If the previous question is ordered on more than one of the pending questions its effect is not exhausted until all of the questions upon which it has been ordered have been voted on, or else the effect of those that have been voted on has been to commit the main question, or to postpone it definitely or indefinitely.

If, before the exhaustion of the previous question, the questions on which it has been ordered that have not been voted on are laid on the table, the previous question is not exhausted thereby, so that when they are taken from the table during the same session, they are still under the previous question and cannot be debated or amended or have any other subsidiary motion applied to them.

Note on the Previous Question.—Much of the confusion heretofore existing in regard to the Previous Question has arisen from the great changes which this motion has undergone. As originally designed, and at present used in the English Parliament, the previous question was not intended to suppress debate, but to suppress the main question, and therefore, in England, it is always moved by the enemies of the measure, who then vote in the negative. It was first used in 1604, and was intended to be applied only to delicate questions; it was put in this form, "Shall the main question be put?" and being negatived, the main question was dismissed for that session. Its form was afterwards changed to this, which is used at present, "Shall the main question be *now* put?" and if negatived the question was dismissed, at first only until after the ensuing debate was over, but now, for that day. The motion for the previous question could be debated; when once put to vote, whether decided affirmatively or negatively, it prevented any discussion of the main question, for, if decided affirmatively, the main question was immediately put, and if decided negatively (that is, that the main question be not now put), it was dismissed for the day.

Our Congress has gradually changed the English Previous Question into an entirely different motion, so that, while in England, the mover of the previous question votes against it, in this country he votes for it. At first the previous question was debatable; if adopted it cut off all motions except the main question, which was immediately put to vote; and if rejected the main question was dismissed for that day as in England. Congress, in 1805, made it undebatable. In 1840 the rule was changed so as not to cut off amendments but to bring the House to a vote first upon pending amendments, and then upon the main question. In 1848 its effect was changed again so as to bring the House to a vote upon the motion to commit if it had been made, then upon amendments reported by a committee, if any, then upon pending amendments, and finally upon the main question. In 1860 Congress decided that the only effect of the previous question, if the motion to postpone were pending, should be to bring the House to a direct vote on the postponement—thus preventing the previous question from cutting off any pending motion. In 1860 the rule was modified also so as to allow it to be applied if so specified to an amendment or to an amendment of an amendment, without affecting anything else, and so that if the previous question were lost the debate would be resumed. In 1880 the rule was further changed so as to allow it to be applied to single motions, or to a series of motions, the motions to which it is to apply being specified in the demand; and 30 minutes' debate, equally divided between the friends and the enemies of the proposition, was allowed after the previous question had been ordered, if there had been no debate previously. In 1890 the 30 minutes' debate was changed to 40 minutes. The previous question now is simply a motion to close debate and proceed to voting on the immediately pending question and such other pending questions as it has been ordered upon.

30. Limit or Extend Limits of Debate. Motions, or orders, to limit or extend the limits of debate, like the previous question, take precedence of all debatable motions, may be applied to any debatable motion or series of motions, and, if not specified to the contrary, apply only to the immediately pending question. If it is voted to limit the debate, the order applies to all incidental and subsidiary motions and the motion to reconsider, subsequently made, as long as the order is in force. But an order extending the limits of debate does not apply to any motions except the immediately pending one and such others as are specified. They are undebatable, and require a two-thirds vote for their adoption. These motions may be amended, but can have no other subsidiary motion applied to them. They yield to privileged [14] and incidental [13] motions, and to the motions to lay on the table and for the previous question. They may be made only when the immediately pending question is debatable. When one of them is pending, another one that does not conflict with it may be moved as an amendment. After one of these motions has been adopted it is in order to move another one of them, provided it does not conflict with the one in force. This motion to limit or extend the limits of debate may be reconsidered even though the order has been partially executed, and if lost it may be renewed after there has been sufficient progress in debate to make it a new question.

After an order is adopted closing debate at a certain hour, or limiting it to a certain time, the motions to postpone and to commit cannot be moved until the vote adopting the order has been reconsidered; but the pending question may be laid on the table, and if it is not taken from the table until after the hour appointed for closing the debate and taking the vote, no debate or motion to amend is allowed, as the chair should immediately put the question. After the adoption of an order limiting the number or length of the speeches, or extending these limits, it is in order to move any of the other subsidiary [12] motions on the pending question.

An order modifying the limits of debate on a question is in force only during the session in which it was adopted. If the question in any way goes over to the next session it is divested of this order and is open to debate according to the regular rules.

The various *Forms* of this motion are as follows:

(1) To fix the hour for closing debate and putting the question, the form is similar to this: "I move that debate close and the question be put on the resolution at 9 P. M."

(2) To limit the length of the debate, the motion may be made thus: "I move that debate on the pending amendment be limited to twenty minutes."

(3) To reduce or increase the number and length of speeches, the motion should be made in a form similar to one of these: "I move that debate on the pending resolution and its amendments be limited to one speech of five minutes from each member;" "I move that Mr. A's time be extended ten minutes;" "I move that Messrs. A and B (the leaders on the two sides) be allowed twenty minutes each, to be divided between their two speeches at their pleasure, and that other members be limited to one speech of two minutes each, and that the question be put at 9 P. M."

31. To Postpone to a Certain Time or Definitely* takes precedence of the motions to commit, to amend, and to postpone indefinitely, and yields to all privileged [14] and incidental [13] motions, and to the motions to lay on the table, for the previous question, and to limit or to extend the limits of debate. It allows of a limited debate which must not go into the merits of the main question any more than is necessary to enable the assembly to determine the propriety of the postponement. It may be amended as to the time, and also by making the postponed question a special order. The previous question and the motions limiting or extending the limits of debate may be applied to it. It cannot be laid on the table alone, but when it is pending the main question may be laid on the table which carries with it the motion to postpone. It cannot be committed or postponed indefinitely. It may be reconsidered. When it makes a question a special order it requires a two-thirds vote.

The time to which a question is postponed must fall within the session or the next session,† and, if it is desired to postpone it to a different time, which must not be beyond the next regular session, it is necessary first to

* In Congress the form of this motion is to postpone to a day certain, unless it is proposed to make the question a special order for a certain hour, when the hour is specified.

† In Congress a motion cannot be postponed to the next session, but it is customary in ordinary societies.

fix the time for an adjourned meeting, and then the question may be postponed to that meeting. Some societies have frequent meetings for literary or other purposes at which business may be transacted, while they hold every month or quarter a meeting especially for business. In such societies these rules apply particularly to the regular business meetings, to which questions may be postponed from the previous regular business meeting or from any of the intervening meetings. Neither the motion to postpone definitely nor an amendment to it, is in order when it has the effect of an indefinite postponement; that is, to defeat the measure, as, for instance, to postpone until tomorrow a motion to accept an invitation to a banquet tonight. If the motion to postpone indefinitely is in order at the time, the chair may treat it as such at his discretion, but it cannot be recognized as a motion to postpone definitely. It is not in order to postpone a class of business, as reports of committees; as each report is announced or called for, it may be postponed, or the rules may be suspended by a two-thirds vote and the desired question be taken up. A matter that is required by the by-laws to be attended to at a specified time or meeting as the election of officers cannot, in advance, be postponed to another time or meeting, but when that specified time or meeting arrives the assembly may postpone it to an adjourned meeting. This is sometimes advisable as in case of an annual meeting for the election of officers occurring on a very stormy night so that a bare quorum is present. After an order of the day or a question of privilege is before the assembly for action, its further consideration may be postponed, or any other subsidiary motion may be applied to it. When a question has been postponed to a certain time, it becomes an order of the day for that time and cannot be taken up before that time except by a reconsideration, or by suspending the rules for that purpose, which requires a two-thirds vote. [See Orders of the Day, **20**, for the treatment of questions that have been postponed definitely.]

The *Form* of this motion depends upon the object sought.

(1) If the object is simply to postpone the question to the next meeting, when it will have precedence of new business, the form of the motion is "to postpone the question [or, that the question be postponed] to the next meeting." It then becomes a general order for that meeting.

(2) If the object is to specify an hour when the question will be taken up as soon as the question then pending, if there is any, is disposed of, the form is similar to this: "I move that the question be postponed to 3 P. M."

(3) If it is desired to postpone the question until after a certain event, when it shall

immediately come up, the form is, "To postpone the question until after the address on Economics."

(4) If the object is to insure its not being crowded out by other matters there should be added to the motion to postpone as given in the first two cases above, the words, "and be made a special order." Or the motion may be made thus: "I move that the question be postponed and made a special order for the next meeting [or, for 3 P. M. tomorrow]." The motion in this form requires a two-thirds vote, as it suspends the rules that may interfere with its consideration at the time specified as explained under Orders of the Day [20].

(5) If it is desired to postpone a question to an adjourned meeting and devote the entire time, if necessary, to its consideration, as in case of revising by-laws, after providing for the adjourned meeting the motion should be made in this form: "I move that the question be postponed and made the special order for next Tuesday evening." Or, a question may be postponed and made the special order for the next regular meeting.

The *Effect* of postponing a question is to make it an order of the day for the time to which it was postponed, and if it is not then disposed of, it becomes unfinished business. Postponing a question to a certain hour does not make it a special order unless so specified in the motion. The motion to postpone definitely may be amended by a majority vote so as to make the amended motion one to make the question a special order. If this is done the amended motion will require a two-thirds vote. [Orders of the Day, **20**, should be read in connection with this section.]

32. To Commit or Refer. (All the rules in regard to this motion, except where stated to the contrary, apply equally to the motions to Go into Committee of the Whole, to Consider Informally, and to Recommit as it is called when a question is committed a second time.) This motion takes precedence of the motions to amend and to postpone indefinitely, and yields to all the other subsidiary [**12**] motions and to all privileged [**14**] and incidental [**13**] motions. It cannot be applied to any subsidiary motion, nor can it be laid on the table or postponed except in connection with the main question. The previous question, and motions to limit or extend the limits of debate, and to amend, may be applied to it without affecting the main question. It is debatable but only as to the propriety of committing the main question.* If the motion to

---

* Congress has changed its rule in regard to the motion to commit, so that now it is undebatable, instead of being debatable and opening to debate the merits of the main question. In a body like Congress, where nearly all the business must be attended to in committees, debate on referring a proposition to a committee should not be allowed. Members can appear before the committee and present their views. But in an ordinary deliberative assembly it is better to observe the general principles governing the debatability of motion as laid down on page 184, and allow of debate as to the propriety of referring the question to a committee.

postpone indefinitely is pending when a question is referred to a committee, it is lost, and is not referred to the committee. Pending amendments go with the main motion to the committee. The motion to commit may be reconsidered, but after the committee has begun the consideration of the question referred to it, it is too late to move to reconsider the vote to commit. The committee may, however, then be discharged as shown below.

The motion to commit (that is, to refer to a committee) may vary in form all the way from the simple form of, "That the question be referred to a committee," to the complete form of referring to question "to a committee of five to be appointed by the chair, with instructions to report resolutions properly covering the case, at the next regular business meeting." If the motion is made in the complete form the details may be changed by amendments, though they are usually treated not as ordinary amendments, but as in filling blanks [page 148].

If the motion is made in the simple form of merely referring the pending question to a committee there are three courses that may be pursued in completing the details, the one to be chosen depending upon the circumstances of the case. (1) The simple, or skeleton, motion may be completed by moving amendments, or making suggestions, for adding the required details as stated below. (2) The chair on his own initiative may call for suggestions to complete the motion, first inquiring as to what committee the question shall be referred, and continuing in the order shown hereafter. (3) The motion in its simplest form may be put to vote at once by its enemies' ordering the previous question, and where the motion to commit is almost certain to be lost this is sometimes done to save the time that would be uselessly spent in completing the details. If it should happen that the motion to commit is adopted, which is improbable, then the details are completed before any new business, except privileged matters, can be taken up. These details are taken up in the order given below, the chair calling for the several items much as if he were completing the motion before it was voted on.

In completing a motion simply to refer to a committee, the first question the chair asks is, "To what committee shall the question be referred?" If different ones are suggested, the suggestions are not treated as amendments of those previously offered, but are voted on in the following order until one receives a majority vote: Committee of the whole; as if in committee of the whole; consider informally; standing committee, in the order in which they are proposed; special (select) committee (largest number voted on first). If the question has already been before a standing or special committee the motion becomes the motion to recommit, and the committees would be voted on in the above order except the old committee would precede other standing and select committees. In suggesting or moving that the committee be a special one, the word "special" is not generally used, the motion being made to refer the question to a committee of five, or any other number, which makes it a special committee; that is, not a standing committee. If any committee except a special one is decided upon, the chair should then put the question on referring the question to that committee. But any one may interrupt him and move to add instructions, or he, himself, may suggest them, or instructions may be given after the vote has been taken on committing the question. Instructions may be given to the committee by a majority vote at any time before it submits its report, even at another session.

If the committee is to be a special one, it is necessary in addition to its number to decide how it is to be appointed. If different methods are suggested, or moved, they are voted on in the following order: Ballot; nominations from the floor (or open nominations); nominations by the chair; and lastly, appointment by the chair, the method that should usually be adopted in very large assemblies. When this is decided the completed motion to commit is put to vote. Instructions as heretofore stated may be added before the vote is taken on the motion to commit, or they may be given afterwards. If the motion to commit is adopted, no new business, except privileged matters, can intervene until the appointment of the committee by the method prescribed, except that when the chair appoints the committee he may wish time to make his selections, which, however, must be announced to the assembly.

If nominations are made from the floor no one can nominate more than one, if objection is made. The member making a nomination in a large assembly rises, and, addressing the chair without waiting to be recognized, says, "I nominate Mr. A." In small assemblies the nominations for committees are frequently made by members from their seats suggesting names. The chair repeats each name as he hears it, and if no more than the prescribed number is suggested, he puts the question on the members named constituting the committee. If more names than the prescribed number are suggested, the chair puts the question on each name in succession, beginning with the first named, until enough are chosen to fill the committee. The negative must be put as well as the affirmative, a majority vote being required for each member of the committee. If the committee is nominated by the chair he states the question thus: "The question is, 'Shall these members constitute the committee?'" It is now in order to move to strike out any of the names, and if such a motion is adopted the chair replaces them with other names. When he appoints the committee no vote is taken, but he must announce the names of the committee to the assembly, and until such announcement is made the committee cannot act. If it is desired to permit the chair to appoint a committee after adjournment, it must be authorized by a vote. The power to appoint a committee carries with it the power to appoint its chairman and to fill any vacancy that may arise in the committee. The resignation of a member of a committee should be addressed to the appointing power.

The *Forms* of this motion are as follows: "To refer the question to a committee;" "To recommit the resolution;" "That the subject be referred to a committee of three to be appointed by the chair, and that it report by resolution at the next meeting;" "That it be referred to a committee with power;" "That the assembly do now resolve itself into [or, go into] committee of the whole, to take under consideration," etc., specifying the subject [55]; "That the resolution be considered as if in committee of the whole" [56]; "That the resolution be considered informally" [57].

The *Object* of the motion to refer to a standing or special committee is usually to enable a question to be more carefully investigated and put into better shape for the assembly to consider, than can be done in the assembly itself. Where an assembly is large and has a very large amount of business it is safer to have every main question go to a committee before final action on it is taken. A special committee to investigate and report upon a subject should consist of representative members on both sides of the question, so that both parties in the assembly may have confidence in the report, or reports in case there is disagreement and a minority report is submitted. By care in selecting committees in ordinary assemblies, debates upon delicate and troublesome questions can be mostly confined to the committees. It is not at all necessary to appoint on the committee the member who makes the motion to refer, but it is usual, and the courteous thing to do, when he is specially interested or informed on the subject. If the appointing power does not designate a chairman of the committee, the member first named acts as such unless the committee elects its own chairman. Consequently it is very important that the first named should be an efficient person, especially in a committee for action.

Sometimes a question is referred to a committee with full power to act in the case. When the duty assigned it has been performed, it should report what it has done, and when this report has been made the committee ceases to exist. When the assembly has decided a question and appoints a committee to take certain action (such as a committee of arrangements for holding a public meeting), then the committee should be small, and all should be favorable to the action to be taken. If any one is appointed on such a committee who is not in sympathy with the proposed action, he should say so and ask to be excused. Sometimes such a committee is given power to add to its number.

The object of going into committee of the whole, or considering a question as if in committee of the whole, or informally, is to enable the assembly to discuss a question with perfect freedom, there being no limit to the number of speeches. The first method is used in the United States House of Representatives, and the second in the United States Senate. The last one is the simplest, and is best adapted to ordinary societies that are not very large. They are explained in **55-57**.

If any form of the motion to commit is made with reference to a question not pending, it becomes a main motion. Thus, a motion to go into committee of the whole on a question not pending, or to appoint a committee upon a subject not pending, or to appoint a committee to take certain action, is a main motion.

To Discharge a Committee. When a committee has made its final report and it has been received by the assembly, the committee ceases to exist without any motion being made to that effect. If, for any reason, the assembly wishes to take a question out of the hands of a committee, and it is too late to reconsider the vote on the committal, it is necessary to "discharge the committee from further consideration" of the resolution or other matter referred to it, for as long as the matter is in the hands of the committee, the assembly cannot consider anything involving practically the same question. If the committee has not yet taken up the question referred to it, the proper motion on the day or the day after it was referred, is to reconsider the vote to commit, which requires only a majority vote. If the motion to reconsider cannot be made, a motion to discharge the committee should be made, which, if adopted, practically rescinds action taken, and therefore requires a two-thirds vote, or a vote of a majority of the membership, unless previous notice of the motion has been given, when it requires only a majority vote. When the committee is discharged its chairman returns to the secretary all papers that have been entrusted to him. It requires a motion to bring the matter referred before the assembly, and this motion may be combined with the motion to discharge, thus: "I move that the committee to whom was referred the resolution on immigration be discharged, and that the resolution be now taken up for consideration [or, be considered at some other specified time]."*

33. To Amend takes precedence of the motion to postpone indefinitely, and yields to all other subsidiary [12] motions and to all privileged [14] and incidental [13] motions, except the motion to divide the question. It can be applied to all motions except those in the *List of Motions that Cannot be Amended* [page 146]. It can be amended itself, but this "amendment of an amendment" (an amendment of the second degree) cannot be amended. The previous question and motions to limit or extend the limits of debate may be applied to an amendment, or to only an amendment of an amendment, and in such case they do not affect the main question, unless so specified. An amendment is debatable in all cases except where the motion to be amended is undebatable. An amendment of a pending question requires only a majority vote for its adoption, even though the question to be amended requires a two-thirds vote. An

---

* In H. R. Rule 27 is the following: "4. Any member may present to the clerk a motion in writing to discharge a committee from further consideration of any public bill or joint resolution which may have been referred to such committee fifteen days prior thereto. All such motions shall be entered in the journal and printed on a calendar to be known as a 'Calendar of Motions to Discharge Committees.' . . . When such motions shall be called up . . . debate on such motion shall be limited to twenty minutes, one-half thereof in favor of the proposition and one-half in opposition thereto. Such motions shall have precedence over motions to suspend the rules and shall require for adoption an affirmative vote of a majority of the membership of the House."

amendment of a constitution or by-laws, or rules of order, or order of business, previously adopted, requires a two-thirds vote; but an amendment of that amendment requires only a majority vote. When a motion or resolution is under consideration only one amendment of the first degree is permitted at a time, and one amendment of that amendment—that is, an amendment of the second degree—is allowed also. An amendment of the third degree would be too complicated and is not in order.* Instead of making it, a member may say that if the amendment of the amendment is voted down, he will offer such and such an amendment of the amendment. While there can be only one amendment of each degree pending at the same time, any number of them may be offered in succession. An amendment must be germane† to the subject to be amended—that is, it must relate to it, as shown further

---

* A substitute may be reported by a committee while amendments of the first and second degree are pending as shown on page 226. In Congress it has been found best to allow a substitute and an amendment thereto while two amendments are pending. The House rule as to amendments is as follows: "When a motion or proposition is under consideration a motion to amend and a motion to amend that amendment shall be in order, and it shall also be in order to offer a further amendment by way of substitute, to which one amendment may be offered, but which shall not be voted on until the original matter is perfected; but either may be withdrawn before amendment or decision is had thereon. Amendments to the title of a bill or resolution shall not be in order until after its passage, and shall be decided without debate." H. R. Rule 19.

† ". . . No motion or proposition on a subject different from that under consideration shall be admitted under color of amendment." H. R. Rule 16, § 7.

on. So an amendment to an amendment must be germane to the latter.

Form. An amendment may be in any of the following forms: (*a*) to *insert* or *add* (that is, place at the end); (*b*) to *strike out;* (*c*) to *strike out* and *insert,* or to *substitute,* as it is called, when an entire paragraph or resolution is struck out and another is inserted. The third form is a combination of the other two and cannot be divided, though, as shown hereafter, for the purposes of amendment the two motions are treated separately, the words to be struck out being first amended and then the words to be inserted. No amendment is in order the effect of which is to convert one of these forms into another.

The motion to amend is made in a form similar to this: "I move to amend the resolution by inserting the word 'very' before the word 'good;'" or, it may be reduced to a form as simple as this: "I move to insert 'very' before 'good.'" The motion to insert should always specify the word before or after which the insertion is to be made. The motion to strike out should also locate the word, provided it occurs more than once. When the chair states the question on the amendment he should repeat the motion in detail so that all may understand what modification is proposed. Unless the effect of the amendment is very evident, he should, in putting the question, show clearly the effect of its adoption, even though it requires the reading of the entire resolution, and then the words to be inserted, or struck out, or struck out and inserted, and finally the resolution as it will stand if the amendment is adopted. He then says, "As many as are in favor of the amendment [or, of striking out, etc., or of inserting, etc.] say *aye;* those opposed, say *no.* The ayes have it, the amendment is adopted, and the question is on the resolution as amended, which is, '*Resolved,* That,'" etc., reading the resolution as amended. If the vote is taken by show of hands or by rising, the question is put and the vote announced thus: "As many as are in favor of the amendment will rise [or, will raise the right hand]; those opposed will rise [or, will manifest it in the same way]. The affirmative has it and the amendment is adopted. The question is on the resolution," etc. The instant the amendment is voted on, whether it is adopted or lost, the chair should announce the result of the vote and state the question that is then before the assembly.

To *Insert* or *Add Words.* When a motion to *insert* [or *add*] certain words is made, the words to be inserted should be perfected by amendments proposed by their friends before the vote is taken on inserting or adding them. After words have been inserted or added, they cannot be changed or struck out except by a motion to strike out the paragraph, or such a portion of it as shall make the question an entirely different one from that of inserting the particular words; or by combining such a motion to strike out the paragraph or a portion of it with the motion to insert other words. The principle involved is that when the assembly has voted that certain words shall form a part of a resolution, it is not in order to make another motion that involves exactly the same question as the one it has decided. The only way to bring it up again is to move to reconsider [36] the vote by which the words were inserted. If the motion to insert is lost, it does not preclude any other motion to insert these words together with other words, or in place of other words, provided the new motion presents essentially a new question to the assembly.

To *Strike out Words.* The motion to strike out certain words can be applied only to consecutive words, though, as the result of amendments, the words may be separated when the final vote is taken. If it is desired to strike out separated words, it is necessary to strike out the separated words by separate motions, or still better, a motion may be made to strike out the entire clause or sentence containing the words to be struck out and insert a new clause or sentence as desired. The motion to strike out certain words may be amended only by striking out words from the amendment, the effect of which is to retain in the resolution the words struck out of the amendment provided both motions are adopted. If the motion to strike out certain words is adopted, the same words cannot be again inserted unless the place or the wording is so changed as to make a new proposition. If the motion to strike out fails,* it does not preclude a motion to strike out the same words and insert other words, or to strike out a part of the words, or to strike out a part and insert other words; or to strike out these words with others, or to do this and insert other words. In each of these cases the new question is materially different from the old one. For striking out all, or a part, of something that has been previously adopted, see "Rescind, etc." [37].

To *Strike Out* and *Insert Words* is a combination of the two preceding motions, and is indivisible.* For purposes of amendment it is resolved into its constituent elements, and the words to be struck out are first amended, after which the words to be inserted are amended. After their amendment the question is put on the motion to strike out and insert. If it is adopted, the inserted words cannot be struck out, nor can the words struck out be inserted, unless the words or place are so changed as to make the question a new one, as described above. If the motion is lost, it does not preclude either of the single motions to strike out

* "A motion to strike out and insert is indivisible, but a motion to strike out being lost shall neither preclude amendment nor motion to strike out and insert; . . ." H. R. Rule 16, §7.

or to insert the same words, nor another motion to strike out and insert, provided there is any material change in either the words to be struck out or the words to be inserted, so that the questions are not practically identical. When it is desired to strike out or modify separated words, a motion may be made to strike out so much of the resolution as is necessary to include all the words to be struck out or changed, and to insert the desired revision including these words. If the words are inserted in the place previously occupied by the words struck out, they may differ materially from the latter, provided they are germane to it. If the words are to be inserted at a different place, then they must not differ materially from those struck out, as it must be in the nature of a transfer The combined motion to strike out words in one place and to insert different words in another place is not in order. Either the place or the words must be substantially the same. If there are several changes to be made, it is usually better to rewrite the paragraph and offer it as a substitute, as shown further on.

Amendments Affecting an Entire Paragraph. A motion to insert (or add) or to strike out a paragraph, or to substitute one paragraph for another, is an amendment of the first degree, and therefore cannot be made when an amendment is pending. The friends of the paragraph to be inserted or struck out should put it in the best possible shape by amending it before it is voted on. After a paragraph has been inserted it cannot be amended except by adding to it; and it cannot be struck out except in connection with other paragraphs so as to make the question essentially a new one. If a paragraph is struck out, it cannot be inserted afterwards unless it is so changed in wording or place as to present an essentially new question. If the motion to insert or to strike out a paragraph is lost, it does not preclude any other motion except one that presents essentially the same question as the one that the assembly has already decided, as shown above in the case of amending words of a paragraph. Thus, when a motion to insert a paragraph has been lost, it is in order to move to insert a part of the paragraph or the entire paragraph if materially altered. So, though the assembly has refused to strike out a paragraph, it is in order to strike out a part of the paragraph or otherwise to amend it, though it is safer for its friends to make it as nearly perfect as possible before the vote is taken on striking it out, with a view to defeating that motion.

A motion to *substitute* one paragraph for another (which is a combination of the two preceding motions) after being stated by the chair is resolved into its two elements for the purpose of amendment, the chair at first entertaining amendments only to the paragraph to be struck out, these amendments being of the second degree. After it is perfected by its friends, the chair asks if there are any amendments proposed to the paragraph to be inserted. When both paragraphs have been perfected by amendments the question is put on substituting one paragraph for the other. Even though the paragraph constitutes the entire resolution and the motion to substitute is carried, it is necessary afterwards to vote on adopting the resolution, as it has only been voted to substitute one paragraph for another. A paragraph that has been substituted for another cannot be amended afterwards, except by adding to it, like any other paragraph that has been inserted. The paragraph that has been replaced cannot be again inserted unless so modified as to constitute a new question, as with any paragraph that has been struck out. If the motion to substitute is lost, the assembly has only decided that that particular paragraph shall not replace the one specified. It may be willing that it replace some other paragraph, or that it be inserted, or that the paragraph retained in the resolution be further amended, or even struck out. But no amendment is in order that presents to the assembly practically a question that it has already decided.

In parliamentary language it is not correct to speak of "substituting" one word or part of a paragraph for another, as the term is applied to nothing less than a paragraph. When a question is being considered by section, it is in order to move a substitute for the pending section. A substitute for the entire resolution, or report, cannot be moved until the sections have all been considered and the chair has announced that the entire paper is open to amendment. When a resolution with amendments of the first and second degree pending, is referred to a committee, they may report it back with a substitute for the resolution which they recommend, even though two amendments are pending. In such a case the chair states the question first on the amendments that were pending when the resolution was committed. When they are disposed of, he states the question on the substitute recommended by the committee and proceeds as in case of any other substitute motion.

Improper Amendments. An amendment is not in order which is not germane to the question to be amended; or merely makes the affirmative of the amended question equivalent to the negative of the original question; or is identical with a question previously decided by the assembly during that session; or changes one form of amendment to another form; or substitutes one form of motion for another form; or strikes out the word *Resolved* from a resolution; or strikes out or inserts words which would leave no rational proposition before the assembly; or is frivolous or absurd. An amendment of an amendment must be germane to—that is, must relate to—the subject of the amendment as well as the main motion. No independent new question can be introduced under cover of an amendment. But an amendment may be in conflict with the spirit of the original motion and still be germane, and therefore in order.

Illustrations: A resolution of censure may be amended by striking out the word "censure" and inserting the word "thanks," for both relate to opinion of certain conduct; refusing to censure is not the same as expressing thanks. A resolution to purchase some books could not be amended by striking out the words relating to books and inserting words relating to a building. Suppose a resolution pending directing the treasurer to purchase a desk for the secretary, and an amendment is offered to add the words, "and to pay the expenses of the delegates to the State Convention;" such an amendment is not germane to the resolution, as paying the expenses of the delegates is in no way related to purchasing a desk for the secretary, and is therefore out of order. But if an amendment were offered to insert the words "and a permanent record book" after the word "desk," it would be in order, because both are articles to enable the secretary to perform his duties. If a resolution were pending condemning certain things, it could be amended by adding other things that were similar or in some way related to them. Suppose a resolution commending A and B for heroism is pending; if the acts of heroism were not connected, amendments are in order adding other names for other acts of heroism; but if the commendation is for an act of heroism in which A and B were joined, then no names can be added to the resolution unless the parties were connected with A and B in that act. Suppose the following resolution pending: "*Resolved*, That the Secretary be instructed to notify our representative in Congress that we do approve of his course in regard to the tariff." A motion to amend by inserting *not* after the word *be* would be out of order, because an affirmative vote on "not instructing" is identical in effect with a negative vote on "instructing." But the motion to insert the word *not* after *do* is in order, for an affirmative vote on disapproving of a certain course is not the same as a negative vote on a resolution of approval, as the latter may mean nothing but an unwillingness to express an opinion on the subject. If a resolution is pending and a member makes the motion, "*I move to strike out the words* 'pine benches' *and insert the words* 'oak chairs,'" it is an amendment of the first degree, and no other amendment of that degree is in order until this is acted upon. All the words in italics are necessary for this form of motion, and are not subject to amendment. The only amendments in order are those that change the words "pine benches" or "oak chairs"—that is, first those to be struck out, and when they are perfected, then those to be inserted. Suppose the motion to *"strike out* 'pine' " is pending, and it is moved to amend by adding *"and insert* 'oak.' " This motion is out of order, as it changes one form of amendment to another form. It is not in order to move to strike out the word "adopt" in a motion and insert the word "reject," as "adopt" is a formal word necessary to show the kind of motion made. Practically, however, the same result may be attained by moving to postpone indefinitely—that is, to reject, the main question. The chair should never rule an amendment out of order unless he is perfectly sure that it is so. If he is in doubt he should admit the amendment, or submit the question as to its being in order to the assembly as described in **21.**

Every original main motion may be amended. All others may be amended, except those contained in the following list of

Motions That Cannot Be Amended.

To adjourn (except when it is qualified, or when made in an assembly with no provision for a future meeting) **17**
Call for the orders of the day **20**
Question of order, and appeal **21**
To object to consideration of a question **23**
Call for a division of the assembly **25**
To grant leave to withdraw a motion **27**

To grant leave to speak after indecorum..... **21**
A request of any kind........................ **27**
To take up a question out of its proper order. **22**
To suspend the rules......................... **22**
To lay on the table.......................... **28**
To take from the table....................... **35**
To reconsider **36**
The previous question........................ **29**
To postpone indefinitely..................... **34**
To amend an amendment........................ **33**
To fill a blank.............................. **33**
A nomination **66**

A motion to adopt a resolution or a by-law may be amended by adding, "and that it be printed and that members be supplied with copies," or, "that they go into effect at the close of this annual meeting," or anything of a similar kind. Under each of the privileged, incidental, and subsidiary motions, it is stated whether or not the motion may be amended, and, when necessary, the way in which it may be amended is explained. An amendment to anything already adopted is not a subsidiary motion. The matter to be amended is not pending and is therefore not affected by anything done with the amendment, provided it is not adopted. Such an amendment is a main motion subject to amendments of the first and second degrees. If the motion is to strike out an entire resolution that has been adopted, it is usually called to *Rescind* and is explained under that head [37]. If the motion is to amend a by-law, etc., it will be found under Amendments of Constitutions, By-laws, etc. [68]. Minutes are usually amended (corrected) informally, the chair directing the correction to be made when suggested. But if objection is made, a formal vote is necessary for the amendment. The minutes may be corrected whenever the error is noticed regardless of the time which has elapsed; but after their adoption, when too late to reconsider the vote, they require a two-thirds vote for their amendment, unless previous notice of the proposed amendment has been given, when only a majority vote is required for its adoption, the same as with the motion to rescind [37]. This is necessary for the protection of the records, which otherwise would be subject to the risk of being tampered with by temporary majorities. The numbers prefixed to paragraphs, articles, etc., are only marginal indications and should be corrected by the secretary, if necessary, without any motion to amend. For amending a long paper, such as a series of resolutions, or a set of by-laws, which should be considered and amended by paragraph, see **24**.

*Filling Blanks.** Propositions for filling blanks are treated somewhat differently from other amendments, in that any number of members may propose, without a second, dif-

---

* While Congress has no rule on filling blanks except the common parliamentary law as laid down in Jefferson's Manual, it rarely makes use of this law, but avails itself of its rule which allows of four amendments pending at the same time, namely, amendments of the first and second degree, and a substitute and amendment to it.

ferent names or numbers for filling the blanks, no one proposing more than one name or number for each place, unless by general consent. These are treated not as amendments, one of another, but as independent propositions to be voted on successively. If the blank is to be filled with a name, the chair repeats the names as they are proposed so all may hear them, and finally takes a vote on each name, beginning with the first proposed, until one receives a majority vote. If the blank is to be filled with several names and no more names are suggested than required, the names may be inserted without a vote. If more names than required are suggested, a vote is taken on each, beginning with the first, until enough to fill the blank have received a majority vote. If the number of names is not specified, a vote is taken on each name suggested, and all that receive a majority vote are inserted.

If the blank is to be filled with a number or a date, then the largest sum, or the longest time, or the most distant date, is put first, unless it is evident to the chair that the reverse order is necessary to enable the first vote to be taken on the proposition that is least likely to be adopted. Suppose a committee is being instructed to purchase a building for a blank amount: the voting on filling the blank should begin with the largest sum proposed; if that is lost, all who voted for it, and some others, would favor the next largest sum, so that the vote would be greater, and so on down to the largest sum that is favored by a majority. If the voting began with the smallest sum, every one would be willing to pay that amount, and it might be adopted and thus cut off voting on the other propositions, whereas a majority would prefer authorizing the committee to spend a larger amount. On the other hand, suppose the committee was being authorized to sell a building for a blank amount: here it is evident that there would be more in favor of the large sum than of the small one. So to get at the wish of the assembly the voting should begin with the smallest sum proposed; all who are willing to sell for that amount, and some additional ones, will be willing to sell for the next larger sum; and so the smallest sum for which the majority is willing to sell will be gradually reached.

It is sometimes convenient to create a blank, as in the following example: A resolution is pending requesting the proper authorities to prohibit the erection of wooden buildings north of A street, and an amendment to strike out A and insert B, and an amendment of the second degree to strike out B and insert C, have been made. The debate developing the fact that several other streets have their advocates, the best course is for the chair to state that, if there is no objection, the motion would be treated as having a blank for the name of the street, and that A, B, and C have been proposed for filling the blank. In this way other names could be suggested and they would be voted on successively beginning with the one that made the prohibited area the largest, and continuing down until one was reached that could get a majority in its favor. If objection is made to leaving a blank for the name, the chair may put the question without waiting for a motion, or any one may move, as an incidental motion, that a blank be created for the name of the street. This motion is undebatable, and cannot be amended, but it may be moved to fill the blank by ballot or in any other way.

The blanks in a resolution should be filled usually before voting on the resolution. But sometimes, when a large majority is opposed to the resolution, the previous question is ordered without waiting for the blanks to be filled, thus stopping debate and further amendment, and bringing the assembly at once to a vote on the resolution. Under such circumstances the resolution would usually be rejected. But should it be adopted, it would be necessary to fill the blanks in the skeleton resolution before any other than privileged business would be in order.

The method adopted in filling blanks has sometimes a great advantage over ordinary amendment. In amending, the last one proposed is the first one voted on, whereas in filling blanks the first one proposed, or nominated, is voted on first, except where, from the nature of the case, another order is preferable, and then that order is adopted as explained above.

Nominations are treated like filling blanks; any number may be pending at the same time, not as amendments of each other, but as independent propositions to be voted on in the order in which they were made until one receives a majority vote. [See 66.]

34. **To Postpone Indefinitely** takes precedence of nothing except the main motion to which it is applied, and yields to all privileged [14], incidental [13], and other subsidiary [12] motions. It cannot be amended or have any other subsidiary motion applied to it except the previous question and motions limiting or extending the limits of debate. It is debatable and opens the main question to debate. It can be applied to nothing but main questions, which include questions of privilege and orders of the day after they are before the assembly for consideration. An affirmative vote on it may be reconsidered, but not a negative vote. If lost it cannot be renewed. It is simply a motion to reject the main question. If a main motion is referred to a committee while to postpone indefinitely is pending, the latter motion is ignored and does not go to the committee.

The *Object* of this motion is not to postpone,

but to reject, the main motion without incurring the risk of a direct vote on it, and it is made only by the enemies of the main motion when they are in doubt as to their being in the majority.

The *Effect* of making this motion is to enable members who have exhausted their right of debate on the main question, to speak again, as, technically, the question before the assembly is different, while, as far as the subject of discussion is concerned, there is no difference caused by changing the question from adopting to rejecting the measure, because the merits of the main question are open to debate in either case. If adopted, its effect is to suppress the main motion for that session, unless the vote is reconsidered. As this motion does not suppress the debate on the main question, its only useful effect is to give the opponents of the pending measure a chance of killing the main motion without risking its adoption in case of failure. For, if they carry the indefinite postponement, the main question is suppressed for the session; if they fail, they still have a vote on the main question, and, having learned their strength by the vote taken, they can form an opinion of the advisability of continuing the struggle.

Art. VI. Some Main and Unclassified Motions.

See **15** for a list of these motions.

35. **To Take from the Table** takes precedence of no pending question, but has the right of way in preference to main motions if made during the session in which it was laid on the table while no question is actually pending, and at a time when business of this class, or unfinished business, or new business, is in order; and also during the next session in societies having regular business meetings as frequently as quarterly. It yields to privileged [**14**] and incidental [**13**] motions, but not to subsidiary [**12**] ones. It is undebatable, and no subsidiary motion can be applied to it. It is not in order unless some business has been transacted since the question was laid on the table, nor can it be renewed until some business has been transacted since it was lost. The motion to take from the table cannot be reconsidered, as it can be renewed repeatedly if lost, and, if carried, the question can be again laid on the table after progress in debate or business.

In ordinary deliberative assemblies, a question is supposed to be laid on the table only temporarily with the expectation of its consideration being resumed after the disposal of the interrupting question, or at a more convenient season.* As soon as the question that was introduced when the first question was laid on the table, is disposed of, any one may move to take this first question from the table. When he rises to make the motion, if the chair recognizes some one else as having first risen, he should at once say that he rises to move to take a question from the table. The chair then assigns him the floor if the other member has risen to make a main motion. If the new main motion has been stated by the chair before he claims the floor, he must wait until that question is disposed of before his motion will be in order. When taken up, the question with everything adhering to it is before the assembly exactly as when it was laid on the table. Thus, if a resolution has amendments and a motion to commit pending at the time it was laid on the table, when it is taken from the table the question is first on the motion to commit. If a motion to postpone to a certain time is pending when the question is laid on the table, and it is taken from the table after that time, then the motion to postpone is ignored when the question is taken up. If the question is taken up on the day it was laid

---

* See foot note on page 107. for the Congressional practice. As stated there, Congress has abandoned the ordinary parliamentary use of the motion to lay on the table and has converted it into a motion to enable the majority to kill a measure instantly. Therefore Congressional practice in regard to laying on, or taking from, the table is of no authority in assemblies using these motions in the common parliamentary law sense.

on the table, members who have exhausted their right of debate cannot again speak on the question. But if taken up on another day, no notice is taken of speeches previously made. The previous question is not exhausted if the question upon which it was ordered is taken from the table at the same session, even though it is on another day.

36. Reconsider.* This motion is peculiar in that the making of the motion has a higher rank than its consideration, and for a certain time prevents anything being done as the result of the vote it is proposed to reconsider. It can be made only on the day the vote to be reconsidered was taken, or on the next succeeding day, a legal holiday or a recess not being counted as a day. It must be made by one who voted with the prevailing side. Any member may second it. It can be made while any other question is pending, even if another member has the floor, or after it has been voted to adjourn, provided the chair has

---

* H. R. Rule 18, §1, is as follows: "1. When a motion has been made and carried, or lost, it shall be in order for any member of the majority, on the same or succeeding day, to move for the reconsideration thereof, and such motion shall take precedence of all other questions except the consideration of a conference report or a motion to adjourn, and shall not be withdrawn after the said succeeding day without the consent of the House, and thereafter any member may call it up for consideration: *Provided*, That such motion, if made during the last six days of a session, shall be disposed of when made." This rule is construed to mean that the motion to reconsider may be made by any member who voted on the question, except when the yeas and nays were ordered to be recorded in the journal, which is done, however, with every important vote.

not declared the assembly adjourned. It may be made after the previous question has been ordered, in which case it and the motion to be reconsidered are undebatable.

While the making of the motion to reconsider has such high privilege, its consideration has only the rank of the motion to be reconsidered, though it has the right of way in preference to any new motion of equal rank, as illustrated further on; and the reconsideration of a vote disposing of a main question either temporarily or permanently may be called up, when no question is pending, even though the general orders are being carried out. The motion to reconsider cannot be amended, postponed indefinitely, or committed. If the reconsideration is laid on the table or postponed definitely, the question to be reconsidered and all adhering questions go with it.* The previous question and the motions limiting or extending the limits of debate may be applied to it when it is debatable. It is undebatable only when the motion to be reconsidered is undebatable. When debatable it opens to de-

---

* In Congress it is usual for the member in charge of an important bill as soon as it is passed to move its reconsideration, and at the same time to move that the reconsideration be laid on the table. If the latter motion is adopted the reconsideration is dead and the bill is in the same condition as if the reconsideration had been voted on and lost. These Rules, like the common parliamentary law, carry the bill to the table, from which it could be taken at any time. [See note, p. 155.] Unless there is a special rule allowing it, the two motions could not be made at the same time in an ordinary society.

bate the merits of the question to be reconsidered. It cannot be withdrawn after it is too late to renew the motion. If the motion to reconsider is lost it cannot be repeated except by general consent. No question can be twice reconsidered unless it was materially amended after its first reconsideration. A reconsideration requires only a majority vote, regardless of the vote necessary to adopt the motion reconsidered.

The motion to reconsider *cannot be applied* to a vote on a motion that may be renewed within a reasonable time; or when practically the same result may be attained by some other parliamentary motion; or when the vote has been partially executed (except in case of the motion to limit debate), or something has been done as the result of the vote that the assembly cannot undo; or to an affirmative vote in the nature of a contract, when the other party to the contract has been notified of the vote; or to a vote on the motion to reconsider. In accordance with these principles, votes on the following motions *cannot be reconsidered:* Adjourn; Take a Recess; Lay on the Table; Take from the Table; Suspend the Rules or Order of Business; and Reconsider. Affirmative votes on the following cannot be reconsidered: Proceed to the Orders of the Day; Adopt, or after they are adopted, to Amend, or Repeal, or Rescind, the Constitution, By-laws, or Rules of Order or any other rules that require previous notice for their amendment; Elect to membership or office if the member or officer is present and does not decline, or if absent and has learned of his election in the usual way and has not declined; to Reopen Nominations. A negative vote on the motion to Postpone Indefinitely cannot be reconsidered as practically the same question comes up again when the vote is taken on the main question. After a committee has taken up the matter referred to it, it is too late to reconsider the vote committing it, though the committee may be discharged. But after debate has proceeded under an order limiting or extending the limits of debate, the vote making that order may be reconsidered, as the debate may develop facts that make it desirable to return to the regular rules of debate. The minutes, or record of proceedings, may be corrected at any time without reconsidering the vote approving them.

If the main question is pending and it is moved to reconsider the vote on any subsidiary [**12**], incidental [**13**], or privileged [**14**] motion, the chair states the question on the reconsideration the moment the motion to be reconsidered is in order if it were made then for the first time. Thus, if, while the motions to commit, for the previous question, and to lay on the table are pending, it is moved to reconsider a negative vote on postponing to a certain time, the chair proceeds to take the vote on laying on the table and, if that is lost, next on the previous question, and then on reconsidering the vote on the postponement, and if that is adopted, then on the postponement, and if that is lost, then on to commit. If the motion to lay on the table had been carried, then when the question was taken from the table the same method of procedure would be followed; that is, the question would be first on ordering the previous question, and next on reconsidering the vote on the postponement, etc. If the reconsideration of an amendment of the first degree is moved while another amendment of the same degree is pending, the pending amendment is first disposed of and then the chair announces the question on the reconsideration of the amendment. If the reconsideration of an amendment to an immediately pending question is moved the chair at once announces the question on the reconsideration.

If the reconsideration is moved while another subject is before the assembly, it cannot interrupt the pending business, but, as soon as that has been disposed of, if called up it has the preference over all other main motions and general orders. In such a case the chair does not state the question on the reconsideration until it is called up.

If the motion to reconsider is made at a time when the reconsideration could be called up if it had been previously made, the chair at once states the question on the reconsideration, unless the mover adds to his motion the words, "and have it entered on the minutes," as explained further on.

If, after the vote has been taken on the adoption of a main motion, it is desired to reconsider the vote on an amendment, it is necessary to reconsider the vote on the main question also, and one motion should be made to cover both votes. The same principle applies in case of an amendment to an amendment, whether the vote has been taken on the resolution, or only on the amendment of the first degree. When the motion covers the reconsideration of two or three votes, the debate is limited to the question that was first voted on. Thus, if the motion is to reconsider the votes on a resolution and amendments of the first and second degree, the debate is limited to the amendment of the second degree. If the motion to reconsider is adopted the chair states the question on the amendment of the second degree and recognizes the mover of the reconsideration as entitled to the floor. The question is now in exactly the same condition it was in just previous to taking the original vote on that amendment.

The *Forms* of making this motion are as follows: "I move to reconsider the vote on the resolution relating to a banquet." "I move to reconsider the vote on the amendment to strike out 'Wednesday' and insert 'Thursday.'" [This form is used when the resolution is still pending.] "I move to reconsider the votes on the resolution relating to a banquet and on the amendment to strike out 'Wednesday' and insert 'Thursday.'" [This form is used when the vote has been taken on the resolution, and it is desired to reconsider the vote on an amendment.] When the motion to reconsider is made the chair states the question, if it can then be considered, and proceeds as with any other question. If it cannot be considered at that time, he says, "Mr. A moves to reconsider the vote on.... .... The secretary will make a note of it," and proceeds with the pending business. The reconsideration, after being moved, is brought before the assembly for action as explained in the previous paragraph. If it is *called up* by a member, he simply says, after obtaining the floor, "I call up the motion to reconsider the vote on.... ...." This call requires no second or vote. If the call is in order, as previously explained, the chair says, "The motion to reconsider the vote [or votes] on.... .... is called up. The question is, 'Will the assembly reconsider the vote [or votes] on......................? Are you ready for the question?'" If the reconsideration is one that the chair states the question on as soon as it can be considered (as when it is moved to reconsider an amendment while another amendment is pending), as soon as the proper time arrives the chair states the question on the reconsideration the same as if the motion to reconsider were made at this time.

When the debate, if there is any, is finished, he *puts the question* thus: "As many as are in favor of reconsidering the vote on the resolution relating to a banquet, say *aye;* those opposed say *no.* The ayes have it and the vote on the resolution is reconsidered. The question is now on the resolution, which is," etc. Or, the question may be put thus: "The question is, Will the assembly reconsider the votes on the resolution relating to a banquet, and on the amendment to strike out 'Wednesday' and insert 'Thursday?' As many as are in favor of the reconsideration say *aye;* those opposed say *no.* The ayes have it and the votes on the resolution and the amendment are reconsidered. The question is now on the amendment, which is," etc. If the motion to reconsider is adopted the business is in exactly the same condition it was in before taking the vote, or the votes, that have been reconsidered, and the chair instantly states the question on the immediately pending question, which is then open to debate and amendment as before.

The *Effect of Making* this motion is to suspend all action that the original motion would have required until the reconsideration is acted upon; but if it is not called up, this effect terminates with the session* [63], except in an assembly having regular meetings as often as quarterly, when, if not called up, its effect does not terminate till the close of the next regular session. As long as its effect lasts, any one at an adjourned, or a special, or a regular meeting, may *call up* the motion to reconsider and have it acted upon, though it is not usual for any one but the mover to call it up on the day it is made if the session lasts beyond that day and there is no need of prompt action.

The *Effect of the Adoption* of this motion is to place before the assembly the original question in the exact position it occupied before it was voted upon; consequently no one, after the reconsideration is adopted, can debate the question reconsidered who had on that day exhausted his right of debate on that question; his only recourse is to discuss the question while the motion to reconsider is before the assembly. If the question is not reconsidered until a later day than that on which the vote to be reconsidered was taken, then it is open to free debate regardless of speeches made previously. When a vote taken under the operation of the previous question is reconsidered, the question is then divested of the pre-

---

* In Congress the effect always terminates with the session, and it cannot be called up by any one but the mover, until the expiration of the time during which it will be in order to move a reconsideration.

vious question, and is open to debate and amendment, provided the previous question had been exhausted by votes taken on all the questions covered by it, before the motion to reconsider was made.

In standing and special committees a vote may be reconsidered regardless of the time elapsed since the vote was taken, provided the motion is made by one who did not vote with the losing side, and that all members who voted with the prevailing side are present, or have received due notice that the reconsideration would be moved at this meeting. A vote cannot be reconsidered in committee of the whole.

*Reconsider and Have Entered on the Minutes.** The motion to reconsider, as previously explained in this section, provides means for correcting, at least on the day on which it occurred, errors due to hasty action. By using the same motion and having it entered on the minutes so that it cannot be called up until another day, a means is provided for preventing a temporary majority from taking action that is opposed by the majority of the society. This is needed in large societies with frequent meetings and small quorums, the at-

---

* In Congress, where the quorum is a majority of the members elected, and the members are paid for their services, there is no need for this form of the motion. On the contrary, it has been found necessary to provide means by which the majority may, when it pleases, prevent the making of the motion to reconsider by any one except the member in charge of the measure.

tendance in many cases not exceeding ten per cent of the membership. It enables a society with a small quorum to protect itself from injudicious action by temporary majorities, without requiring previous notice of main motions and amendments as is done in the English Parliament. To accomplish this, however, it is necessary to allow this form of the motion to be applied to a vote finally disposing of a main motion, regardless of the fact that the motion to reconsider has already been made. Otherwise it would be useless, as it would generally be forestalled by the motion to reconsider, in its simple form, which would be voted down, and then this motion could not be made. As this form of the motion is designed only to be used when the meeting is an unrepresentative one, this fact should be very apparent, and some members of the temporary minority should vote with the temporary majority on adopting or postponing indefinitely a main motion of importance, when they think the action is in opposition to the wishes of the great majority of the society. One of them should then move "to reconsider the vote on the resolution [or motion] and have it [or, request that it be] entered on the minutes," which has the effect of suspending all action required by the vote it is proposed to reconsider, as previously explained, and thus gives time to notify absent members of the proposed action. If no member of the temporary minority voted with the majority, and it is too late for any one to change his vote so as to move to reconsider, then some one should give notice of a motion to rescind the objectionable vote at the next meeting, which may be done by a majority vote after this notice has been given.

Should a minority make an improper use of this form of the motion to reconsider by applying it to a vote which required action before the next regular business meeting, the remedy is at once to vote that when the assembly adjourns it adjourns to meet on another day, appointing a suitable day, when the reconsideration could be called up and disposed of. The mere making of this motion would probably cause the withdrawal of the motion to reconsider, as it would defeat the object of that motion if the majority of the society is in favor of the motion to be reconsidered. If the motion to reconsider is withdrawn, of course the other would be.

This form of the motion to reconsider and have entered on the minutes differs from the simple form to reconsider in the following respects:

(1) It can be made only on the day the vote to be reconsidered is taken. If a meeting is held on the next day the simple form of the motion to reconsider, made then, accomplishes the object of this motion by bringing the question before the assembly on a

different day from the one when the vote was taken.

(2) It outranks the simple form of the motion to reconsider, and may be made even after the vote has been taken on the motion to reconsider, provided the result of the vote has not been announced. If made after the simple form of the motion to reconsider, it supersedes the latter, which is thereafter ignored.

(3) It can be applied only to votes which finally dispose of the main question. They are as follows: an affirmative or negative vote on adopting, and an affirmative vote on postponing indefinitely, a main question. And it may be applied to a negative vote on the consideration of a question that has been objected to, provided the session extends beyond that day.

(4) In an assembly not having regular business meetings as often as quarterly, it cannot be moved at the last business meeting of a session.

(5) It cannot be called up on the day it is made, except when it is moved on the last day of a session of an assembly not having regular business sessions as often as quarterly, when any one can call it up at the last business meeting of the session.

After it is called up there is no difference in the treatment of the two forms of the motion.

37. Rescind, Repeal, or Annul. Any vote taken by an assembly, except those mentioned further on, may be rescinded by a majority vote, provided notice of the motion has been given at the previous meeting or in the call for this meeting; or it may be rescinded without notice by a two-thirds vote, or by a vote of a majority of the entire membership. The notice may be given when another question is pending, but cannot interrupt a member while speaking. To rescind is identical with the motion to amend something previously adopted, by striking out the entire by-law, rule, resolution, section, or paragraph, and is subject to all the limitations as to notice and vote that may be placed by the rules on similar amendments. It is a main motion without any privilege, and therefore can be introduced only when there is nothing else before the assembly. It cannot be made if the question can be reached by calling up the motion to reconsider which has been previously made. It may be made by any member; it is debatable, and yields to all privileged and incidental motions; and all of the subsidiary motions may be applied to it. The motion to rescind can be applied to votes on all main motions, including questions of privilege and orders of the day that have been acted upon, and to votes on an appeal, with the following *exceptions:* votes cannot be rescinded after something has been done as a result of that vote that the assembly cannot undo; or where it is in the nature of a contract and the other party is informed of the fact; or, where a resignation has been acted upon, or one has been elected to, or expelled from, membership or office, and was present or has been officially notified. In the case of expulsion, the only way to reverse the action afterwards is to restore the person to membership or office, which requires the same preliminary steps and vote as is required for an election.

Where it is desired not only to rescind the action, but to express very strong disapproval, legislative bodies have, on rare occasions, voted to rescind the objectionable resolution and *expunge* it from the record, which is done by crossing out the words, or drawing a line around them, and writing across them the words, "Expunged by order of the assembly," etc., giving the date of the order. This statement should be signed by the secretary. The words expunged must not be so blotted as not to be readable, as otherwise it would be impossible to determine whether more was expunged than ordered. Any vote less than a majority of the total membership of an organization is certainly incompetent to expunge from the records a correct statement of what was done and recorded and the record of which was officially approved, even though a quorum is present and the vote to expunge is unanimous.

38. Renewal of a Motion. When an original main motion or an amendment has been adopted, or rejected, or a main motion has been postponed indefinitely, or an objection to its consideration has been sustained, it, or practically the same motion, cannot be again brought before the assembly at the same session, except by a motion to reconsider or to rescind the vote. But it may be introduced again at any future session.

In assemblies having regular sessions as often at least as quarterly, a main motion cannot be renewed until after the close of the next regular session, if it was postponed to that next session; or laid on the table; or adopted, or rejected, or postponed indefinitely, and the motion to reconsider was made and not acted on at the previous session. In these cases the question can be reached at the next session at the time to which it was postponed, or by taking it from the table, or by reconsidering the vote.

In assemblies whose regular sessions are not as frequent as quarterly, any motion which has not been committed or postponed to the next session may be renewed at that next session. The motions to adjourn, to take a recess, and to lay on the table, may be made again and again, provided there has been progress in debate or business, but the making of, or voting on, these motions is not business that justifies the renewal of a motion. Neither a motion to postpone indefinitely nor an amendment can be renewed at the same session, but the other subsidiary motions may be renewed whenever the progress in debate or business is such as to make the question before the assembly practically a different one. To take from the table and a call for the orders of the day may be renewed after the business is disposed of that was taken up when the motion to take from the table, or for the orders of the day, was lost. To postpone indefinitely cannot be renewed even though the main motion has been amended since the indefinite postponement was previously moved. A point of order cannot be raised if an identical one has been raised previously without success during the same session. And after the chair has been sustained in a ruling he need not entertain an appeal from a similar decision during the same session. Minutes may be corrected regardless of the time elapsed and of the fact that the correction had been previously proposed and lost.

When a subject which has been referred to a committee is reported back at the same meeting, or a subject that has been laid on the table is taken up at the same meeting, it is not a renewal.

The following motions, unless they have been withdrawn, *cannot be renewed* at the same session: to adopt or postpone indefinitely an original main motion; to amend; to reconsider, unless the question to be reconsidered was amended materially when previously reconsidered; to object to the consideration of a question; to fix the same time to which to adjourn; to suspend the rules for the same purpose at the same meeting, though it may be renewed at another meeting held the same day.

It is the duty of the chair to prevent the privilege of renewal from being used to obstruct business, and when it is evident that it is being so misused he should protect the assembly by refusing to recognize the motions, as explained under Dilatory Motions [40].

39. **Ratify.** This is a main motion and is used when it is desired to confirm or make valid some action which requires the approval of the assembly to make it valid. The assembly may ratify only such actions of its officers or committees, or delegates, as it had the right to authorize in advance. It cannot make valid a viva voce election when the by-laws require it to be by ballot, nor can it ratify anything done in violation of the laws of the state, or of its own constitution or by-laws, except that it may ratify emergency action taken at a meeting when no quorum was present, even though the quorum is provided for in a by-law. A motion to ratify may be amended by substituting a motion of censure, and vice versa, when the action has been taken by an officer or other representative of the

assembly. It is debatable and opens the entire question to debate.

40. Dilatory, Absurd, or Frivolous Motions. For the convenience of deliberative assemblies, it is necessary to allow some highly privileged motions to be renewed again and again after progress in debate or the transaction of any business, and to allow a single member, by calling for a division, to have another vote taken. If there was no provision for protecting the assembly, a minority of two members could be constantly raising questions of order and appealing from every decision of the chair, and calling for a division on every vote, even when it was nearly unanimous, and moving to lay motions on the table, and to adjourn, and offering amendments that are simply frivolous or absurd. By taking advantage of parliamentary forms and methods a small minority could practically stop the business of a deliberative assembly having short sessions, if there was no provision for such contingency. Congress met it by adopting this rule: "No dilatory motion shall be entertained by the speaker." But, without adopting any rule on the subject, every deliberative assembly has the inherent right to protect itself from being imposed upon by members using parliamentary forms to prevent it from doing the very thing for which it is in session, and which these forms were designed to assist, namely, to transact business. Therefore, whenever the chair is satisfied that members are using parliamentary forms merely to obstruct business, he should either not recognize them, or else rule them out of order. After the chair has been sustained upon an appeal, he should not entertain another appeal from the same obstructionists while they are engaged evidently in trying by that means to obstruct business. While the chair should always be courteous and fair, he should be firm in protecting the assembly from imposition, even though it be done in strict conformity with all parliamentary rules except this one, that no dilatory, absurd, or frivolous motions are allowed.

As an illustration of a frivolous or absurd motion, suppose Mr. A is to be in the city next week and a motion has been made to invite him to address the assembly at its next meeting, the meetings being weekly. Now, if a motion is made to refer the question to a committee with instructions to report at the next regular meeting, the chair should rule it out of order as frivolous or absurd.

41. Call of the House.* (This cannot be used in ordinary assemblies, as they have not the power to compel the attendance of members.)

---

* In the early history of our Congress a call of the house required a day's notice, and in the English Parliament it is usual to order that the call shall be made on a certain day in the future, usually not over ten days afterwards, though it has been as long as six weeks afterwards. The object of this is to give notice so that all the members may be present on that day, when important business is to come before the house. In Congress a call

The object of a call of the house is to compel the attendance of absent members, and is allowable only in assemblies that have the power to compel the attendance of absentees. It is usual to provide in such assemblies that when no quorum is present, a specified small number can order a call of the house. In Congress a call of the house may be ordered by a majority vote, provided one-fifth of the members elect are present. A rule like the following would answer for city councils and other similar bodies that have the power to enforce attendance.

Rule. When no quorum is present, if one-fifth of the members elect are present, they may by a majority vote order a call of the house and compel the attendance of absent members. After the call is ordered, a motion to adjourn, or to dispense with further proceedings in the call, cannot be entertained until a quorum is present, or until the sergeant-at-arms* reports that in his opinion no quorum can be obtained on that day.

If no quorum is present, a call of the house takes precedence of everything, even reading the minutes, except the motion to adjourn, and only requires in its favor the number specified in the rule. If a quorum is present a call should rank with questions of privilege [19], requiring a majority vote for its adoption, and if rejected it should not be renewed while a quorum is present at that meeting. After a call is ordered, until further proceedings in the call are dispensed with, no motion is in order except to adjourn and a motion relating to the call, so that a recess could not be taken by unanimous consent. An adjournment puts an end to all proceedings in the call, except that the assembly before adjournment, if a quorum is present, can order such members as are already

---

of the house is only used now when no quorum is present, and as soon as a quorum appears it is usual to dispense with further proceedings in the call, and this is in order at any stage of the proceedings. In Congress it is customary afterwards to remit the fees that have been assessed. In some of our legislative bodies proceedings in the call cannot be dispensed with except a majority of the members elect to vote in favor of so doing.

* The term sergeant-at-arms should be replaced by "chief of police," or the title of whatever officer serves the warrant.

arrested to make their excuse at an adjourned meeting.

Proceedings in a Call of the House. When the call is ordered the clerk calls the roll of members alphabetically, noting the absentees; he then calls over again the names of absentees, when excuses* can be made; after this the doors are locked, no one being permitted to leave, and an order similar in form to the following is adopted: *"Ordered,* That the sergeant-at-arms take into custody, and bring to the bar of the House, such of its members as are absent without the leave of the House." A warrant signed by the presiding officer and attested by the clerk, with a list of absentees attached, is then given to the sergeant-at-arms, who immediately proceeds to arrest the absentees. When he appears with members under arrest, he proceeds to the chairman's desk (being announced by the doorkeeper in large bodies), followed by the arrested members, and makes his return. The chairman arraigns each member separately, and asks what excuse he has to offer for being absent from the sittings of the assembly without its leave. The member states his excuse, and a motion is made that he be discharged from custody and admitted to his seat either without payment of fees or after paying his fees. Until a member has paid the fees assessed against him he cannot vote or be recognized by the chair for any purpose.

Art. VII. Debate.

PAGE

* It is usual in Congress to excuse those who have "paired off," that is, two members on opposite sides of the pending question who have agreed that while one is absent the other will not vote on the question. Pairing should not be allowed on questions requiring a two-thirds vote.

42. Debate. In **1-6** are explained the necessary steps preliminary to debate—namely, that when no business is pending a member shall rise and address the chair by his title, and be recognized by the chair as having obtained the floor; and that the member shall then make a motion which, after being seconded, shall be stated by the chair, who shall then ask, "Are you ready for the question?" The question is then open to debate, as is partially explained in **7**, which should be read in connection with this section. No member shall speak more than twice during the same day to the same question (only once on an appeal), nor longer than ten minutes at one time, without leave of the assembly; and the question upon granting the leave shall be decided by a two-thirds vote without debate.* No member can speak a second time to a question as long as any member desires to speak who has not spoken to the question. If greater freedom is desired, the proper course is to go into committee of the whole, or to consider it informally, either of which requires only a majority vote; or to extend the limits of debate [**30**],

* The limit of time should vary to suit circumstances, but the limit of two speeches of ten minutes each will usually answer in ordinary assemblies, and, when desirable, by a two-thirds vote it can be increased or diminished as shown in **30**. In the U. S. House of Representatives no member can speak more than once to the same question, nor longer than one hour. In the Senate there is no limit to the length of a speech, and no senator can speak more than twice on the same day to the same question without leave of the Senate, which question is undebatable.

which requires a two-thirds vote. So the debate, by a two-thirds vote, may be limited to any extent desired, as shown in **30**. The member upon whose motion the subject was brought before the assembly, is entitled to close the debate with a speech, if he has not previously exhausted his twenty minutes, but not until every one else wishing to speak has spoken. He cannot, however, avail himself of this privilege after debate has been closed.* An amendment, or any other motion, being offered, makes the real question before the assembly a different one, and, in regard to the right to debate, is treated as a new question. When an amendment is pending the debate must be confined to the merits of the amendment, unless it is of such a nature that its decision practically decides the main question. Merely asking a question, or making a suggestion, is not considered as speaking. The maker of a motion, though he can vote against it, cannot speak against his own motion. [To close the debate see **44**.]

The right of members to debate and make motions cannot be cut off by the chair's putting a question to vote with such rapidity as to prevent the member's getting the floor after the chair has inquired if the assembly is ready for the question. Even after the chair has

* Formerly the member who reported a proposition from a committee was permitted to close the debate in the House after the previous question was ordered, provided he had not used all of his hour previously.

announced the vote, if it is found that a member arose and addressed the chair with reasonable promptness after the chair asked, "Are you ready for the question?" he is then entitled to the floor, and the question is in exactly the same condition it was before it was put to vote. But if the chair gives ample opportunity for members to claim the floor before putting the question and they do not avail themselves of it, they cannot claim the right of debate after the voting has commenced.

43. Decorum in Debate. In debate a member must confine himself to the question before the assembly, and avoid personalities. He cannot reflect upon any act of the assembly, unless he intends to conclude his remarks with a motion to rescind such action, or else while debating such a motion. In referring to another member, he should, as much as possible, avoid using his name, rather referring to him as "the member who spoke last," or in some other way describing him. The officers of the assembly should always be referred to by their official titles. It is not allowable to arraign the motives of a member, but the nature or consequences of a measure may be condemned in strong terms. It is not the man, but the measure, that is the subject of debate.

If one desires to ask a question of the member speaking, he should rise, and without waiting to be recognized, say, "Mr. Chairman, I should like to ask the gentleman a question." The chair then asks the speaker if he is willing to be interrupted, or the speaker may at once consent or decline, addressing, however, the chair, through whom the conversation must be carried on, as members cannot directly address one another in a deliberative assembly. If the speaker consents to the question, the time consumed by the interruption comes out of the time of the speaker.

If at any time the chairman rises to state a point of order, or give information, or otherwise speak, within his privilege, the member speaking must take his seat till the chairman has been heard first. When called to order by the chair the member must sit down until the question of order is decided. If his remarks are decided to be improper, he cannot proceed, if any one objects, without the leave of the assembly expressed by a vote, upon which question no debate is allowed.

Disorderly words should be taken down by the member who objects to them, or by the secretary, and then read to the member. If he denies them, the assembly shall decide by a vote whether they are his words or not. If a member cannot justify the words he used, and will not suitably apologize for using them, it is the duty of the assembly to act in the case. If the disorderly words are of a personal nature, after each party has been heard, and before the assembly proceeds to deliberate upon the case, both parties to the personality should retire, it being a general rule that no member should be present in the assembly when any matter relating to himself is under debate. It is not, however, necessary for the member objecting to the words to retire unless he is personally involved in the case. Disorderly words to the presiding officer, or in respect to the official acts of an officer, do not involve the officer so as to require him to retire. If any business has taken place since the member spoke, it is too late to take notice of any disorderly words he used.

During debate, and while the chairman is speaking, or the assembly is engaged in voting, no member is permitted to disturb the assembly by whispering, or walking across the floor, or in any other way.

44. Closing Debate and Preventing Debate. When the debate appears to the chairman to be finished, he should inquire, "Are you ready for the question?" If, after a reasonable pause, no one rises to claim the floor, the chair assumes that no member wishes to speak and, standing, proceeds to put the question. Debate is not closed by the chairman's rising and putting the question, as until both the affirmative and the negative are put, a member can rise and claim the floor, and reopen the debate or make a motion, provided he rises with reasonable promptness after the chair asks, "Are you ready for the question?" If the debate is resumed the question must be put again, both the affirmative and the negative. Should this privilege be abused by members not responding to the inquiry, "Are you ready for the question?" and intentionally waiting until the affirmative vote has been taken and then rising and reopening the debate, the chair should act as in case of dilatory motions [40], or any other attempt to obstruct business, and protect the assembly from annoyance. When a vote is taken a second time, as when a division is called for, debate cannot be resumed except by general consent.

If two-thirds of the assembly wish to close the debate without allowing all the time desired by others, they can do so by ordering either the previous question or the closing of the debate at a certain time; or they can limit the length of the speeches and allow each member to speak only once on each question, as fully explained in 29 and 30. These motions require a two-thirds* vote, as they sus-

* In the Senate not even two-thirds of the members can force a measure to its passage without allowing debate, the Senate rules not recognizing the above motions. In the House, where each speaker can occupy the floor one hour, any of these motions to cut off debate can be adopted by a mere majority, but practically they are not used until after some debate. Rule 27, §3, H. R., expressly provides that forty minutes, twenty on each side, shall be allowed for debate whenever the previous question is ordered on a proposition on which there has been no debate, or when the rules are suspended. [See note to **22.**] In ordinary societies harmony is so essential that a two-thirds vote should be required to force the assembly to a final vote without allowing free debate.

pend the fundamental right of every member of a deliberative assembly to have every question fully discussed before it is finally disposed of. A majority vote may lay the question on the table and thus temporarily suspend the debate, but it can be resumed by taking the question from the table by a majority vote when no question is before the assembly [35], at a time when business of this class, or unfinished business, or new business, is in order. If it is desired to prevent any discussion of a subject, even by its introducer, the only way to do it is to object to the consideration of the question [23] before it is debated, or any subsidiary motion is stated. If the objection is sustained by a two-thirds vote, the question is thrown out for that session.

45. Principles of Debate and Undebatable Motions. All main motions are debatable, and debate is allowed or prohibited on other motions in accordance with the following principles:

(*a*) *High privilege is, as a rule, incompatible with the right of debate of the privileged motion:* and, therefore, all highly privileged motions are undebatable, except those relating to the privileges of the assembly or a member. Questions of privilege [19] rarely arise, but when they do, they are likely to be so important that they must be allowed to interrupt business, and yet they cannot generally be acted upon intelligently without debate.

and, therefore, they are debatable. The same is true of appeals from the decision of the chair which are debatable, unless they relate to indecorum, or to transgression of the rules of speaking, or to priority of business, or are made while an undebatable question is pending; in which cases there is not sufficient need of debate to justify making them an exception to the rule, and therefore an appeal under any of these circumstances is undebatable.

(*b*) *Motions that have the effect of suspending a rule are not debatable.* Consequently motions to suppress, or to limit, or to extend the limits of, debate are undebatable, as they suspend the ordinary rules of debate.

(*c*) Appeals made after the previous question has been ordered are undebatable, as it would be manifestly improper to permit debate on them when the assembly by a two-thirds vote has closed debate on the pending question. So any order limiting debate on the pending question applies to questions arising while the order is in force.

(*d*) To Amend, or to Reconsider, an undebatable question is undebatable, whereas to amend, or to reconsider, a debatable question is debatable.

(*e*) *A Subsidiary Motion* [12] is debatable to just the extent that it interferes with the right of the assembly to take up the original question at its pleasure. *Illustrations:* To

"Postpone Indefinitely" a question places it out of the power of the assembly to again take it up during that session, except by reconsideration, and consequently this motion allows of free debate, even involving the whole merits of the original question. To "Commit" a question only delays the discussion until the committee reports, when it is open to free debate, so it is only debatable as to the propriety of the commitment and as to the instructions, etc. To "Postpone to a Certain Time" prevents the consideration of the question till the specified time, except by a reconsideration or suspension of the rules, and therefore allows of limited debate upon the propriety of the postponement. To "Lay on the Table" leaves the question so that the assembly can consider it at any time that that question or that class of business is in order, and therefore to lay on the table should not be, and is not, debatable.

Because a motion is undebatable it does not follow that while it is pending the chair may not permit a question or an explanation. The distinction between debate and asking questions or making brief suggestions, should be kept clearly in mind, and when the latter will aid the assembly in transacting business, the chair should permit it before taking the vote on an undebatable question. He should, however, remain standing during the colloquy to show that he has the floor, and he should not allow any more delay in putting the question than he feels is helpful to the business.

The following lists of motions that open the main question to debate, and of those that are undebatable, are made in accordance with the above principles:

Motions That Open the Main Question to Debate.

Postpone Indefinitely........................ 34
Reconsider a Debatable Question............ 36
Rescind 37
Ratify 39

Undebatable Motions.

Fix the Time to which to Adjourn (when a privileged question) 16
Adjourn (when unqualified in an assembly that has provided for future meetings).... 17
Take a Recess (when privileged)............ 18
Call for the Orders of the Day, and questions relating to priority of business............ 20
Appeal when made while an undebatable question is pending, or when simply relating to indecorum, or transgression of the rules of speaking, or to priority of business........ 21
Suspension of the Rules.................... 22
Objection to the Consideration of a Question. 23
Incidental Motions, except an Appeal as shown above in this list under Appeal............. 13
Lay on the Table.......................... 28
Previous Question [29] and *Motiors to Close, Limit, or Extend the Limits of Debate*..... 30
Amend an Undebatable Motion.............. 33
Reconsider an Undebatable Motion.......... 36

Art. VIII. Vote.

46. Voting. If the question is undebatable, or debate has been closed by order of the assembly, the chair, immediately after stating the question, puts it to vote as described under Putting the Question [9], only allowing time for members to rise if they wish to make a motion of higher rank.

If the question is debatable and no one rises to claim the floor, after the question is stated by the chair, he should inquire, "Are you ready for the question?" After a moment's pause, if no one rises, he should put the question to vote. If the question is debated or motions are made, the chair should wait until the debate has apparently ceased, when he should again inquire, "Are you ready for the question?" Having given ample time for any one to rise and claim the floor, and no one having done so, he should put the question to vote and announce the result.

The usual method of taking a vote is *viva voce* (by the voice). The rules require this method to be used in Congress. In small assemblies the vote is often taken by "show of hands," or by "raising the right hand" as it is also called. The other methods of voting are by rising; by ballot; by roll call, or "yeas and nays," as it is also called; by general consent; and by mail. In voting by any of the first three methods, the affirmative answer *aye*, or raise the right hand, or rise, as the case may be: then the negative answer *no*, or raise the right hand, or rise.

The responsibility of announcing, or declaring, the vote rests upon the chair, and he, therefore, has the right to have the vote taken again, by rising, if he is in doubt as to the result, and even to have the vote counted, if necessary. He cannot have the vote taken by ballot or by yeas and nays (roll call) unless it is required by the rules or by a vote of the assembly. But if the viva voce vote does not make him positive as to the result he may at once say, "Those in favor of the motion will rise;" and when they are seated he will continue, "Those opposed will rise." If this does not enable him to determine the vote, he should say, "Those in favor of the motion [or, Those in the affirmative] will rise and stand until counted." He then counts those standing, or directs the secretary to do so, and then says, "Be seated. Those opposed [or, Those in the negative] rise and stand until counted." After both sides are counted the chair announces the result as shown below. In a very large assembly the chair may find it necessary to appoint tellers to count the vote and report to him the numbers. In small assemblies a show of hands may be substituted for a rising vote.

When the vote is taken by voice or show of hands any member has a right to require a *division of the assembly* [25] by having the affirmative rise and then the negative, so that all may see how members vote. Either before or after a decision any member may call for, or demand, a count, and, if seconded, the chair must put the question on ordering a count. In organizations where it is desired to allow less than a majority vote to order a count or tellers, a special rule should be adopted specifying the necessary vote. Where no rule has been adopted a majority vote is required to order a count, or that the vote be taken by ballot or by yeas and nays (roll call).

Announcing the Vote. When the vote has been taken so that the chair has no doubt as to the result, and no division is called for, or, if so, the assembly has divided, the chair proceeds to announce, or declare the vote thus: "The ayes have it and the resolution is adopted." If he is not very positive, he may say, "The ayes seem to have it," and, if no one says he doubts the vote or calls for a division, after a slight pause he adds, "The ayes have it," etc. If the vote was by show of hands or by rising, it would be announced thus: "The affirmative has it (or, the motion is carried) and the question is laid on the table;"

or if there was a count, the vote would be announced thus: "There are 95 votes in the affirmative, and 99 in the negative, so the amendment is lost, and the question is now on the resolution; are you ready for the question?" In announcing a vote the chair should state first whether the motion is carried or lost; second, what is the effect, or result, of the vote; and third, what is the immediately pending question or business, if there is any. If there is none, he should ask, "What is the further pleasure of the assembly?" One of the most prolific causes of confusion in deliberative assemblies is the neglect of the chair to keep the assembly well informed as to what is the pending business. The habit of announcing the vote by simply saying that the "motion is carried" and then sitting down, cannot be too strongly condemned. Many members may not know what is the effect of the vote, and it is the chair's duty to inform the assembly what is the result of the motion's being carried or lost, and what business comes next before the assembly.

When a quorum [64] is present, a majority vote, that is a majority of the votes cast, ignoring blanks, is sufficient for the adoption of any motion that is in order, except those mentioned in 48, which require a two-thirds vote. A plurality never adopts a motion nor elects any one to office, unless by virtue of a special rule previously adopted. On a tie vote the motion is lost, and the chair, if a member of the assembly, may vote to make it a tie unless the vote is by ballot. The chair cannot, however, vote twice, first to make a tie and then give the casting vote. In case of an appeal [21], though the question is, "Shall the decision of the chair stand as the judgment of the assembly?" a tie vote, even though his vote made it a tie, sustains the chair, upon the principle that the decision of the chair can be reversed only by a majority, including the chair if a member of the assembly.

It is a general rule that no one can vote on a question in which he has a direct personal or pecuniary interest. Yet this does not prevent a member from voting for himself for any office or other position, as voting for a delegate or for a member of a committee; nor from voting when other members are included with him in the motion, even though he has a personal or pecuniary interest in the result, as voting on charges preferred against more than one person at a time, or on a resolution to increase the salaries of all the members. If a member could in no case vote on a question affecting himself, it would be impossible for a society to vote to hold a banquet, or for a legislature to vote salaries to members, or for the majority to prevent a small minority from preferring charges against them and suspending or expelling them. By simply including the names of all the members, except those of their own faction, in a resolution preferring charges against them, the minority could get all the power in their own hands, were it not for the fact that in such a case all the members are entitled to vote regardless of their personal interest. A sense of delicacy usually prevents a member from exercising this right of voting in matters affecting himself except where his vote might affect the result. After charges are preferred against a member, and the assembly has ordered him to appear for trial, he is theoretically under arrest, and is deprived of all rights of membership and therefore cannot vote until his case is disposed of.

A member has the right to change his vote up to the time the vote is finally announced. After that, he can make the change only by permission of the assembly, which may be given by general consent; that is, by no member's objecting when the chair inquires if any one objects. If objection is made, a motion may be made to grant the permission, which motion is undebatable.

While it is the duty of every member who has an opinion on the question to express it by his vote, yet he cannot be compelled to do so. He may prefer to abstain from voting, though he knows the effect is the same as if he voted on the prevailing side.

Voting by Ballot. The main object of this form of voting is secrecy, and it is resorted to when the question is of such a nature that some members might hesitate to vote publicly their true sentiments. Its special use is in the reception of members, elections, and trials of members and officers, as well as in the preliminary steps in both cases, and the by-laws should require the vote to be by ballot in such cases. Where the by-laws do not require the vote to be by ballot, it can be so ordered by a majority vote, or by general consent. Such motions are undebatable. Voting by ballot is rarely, if ever, used in legislative bodies, but in ordinary societies, especially secret ones, it is habitually used in connection with elections and trials, and sometimes for the selection of the next place for the meeting of a convention. As the usual object of the ballot is secrecy, where the by-laws require the vote to be taken by ballot any motion is out of order which members cannot oppose without exposing their views on the question to be decided by ballot. Thus, it is out of order to move that one person cast the ballot of the assembly for a certain person when the by-laws require the vote to be by ballot. So, when the ballot is not unanimous it is out of order to move to make the vote unanimous, unless the motion is voted on by ballot so as to allow members to vote against it in secrecy.

In some cases black balls and white ones and a ballot box are provided for voting, where the question can be answered *yes* or *no*. The white ball answers *yes*, and the black one *no*. But in ordinary deliberative assemblies the ballots are strips of paper upon which are printed, or written, *yes* or *no,* or the names of the candidates, as the case may be. These ballots are first distributed and are afterwards collected by tellers, either by being dropped into a hat or box by the members, who remain in their seats; or by the members coming to the ballot box and handing their folded ballot to a teller, who deposits it in the ballot box. In the latter case it is necessary for the tellers to see that no member votes twice, which in large societies can be best done by checking off the names from a list of members as the ballots are deposited. The ballots should usually be folded so that if more than one is voted by the same person the tellers will detect it in unfolding the ballot. In satisfying themselves that only one ballot is voted, the vote may be exposed if the ballot is not folded.

When every one appears to have voted, the chair inquires, "Have all voted who wish to?" and if there is no response he says, "The polls are closed," whereupon the tellers proceed to count the ballots. If in unfolding the ballots it is found that two have been folded together, both are rejected as fraudulent. A blank piece of paper is not counted as a ballot and would not cause the rejection of the ballot with which it was folded. All blanks are ignored as simply waste paper, and are not reported, the members who do not wish to vote adopting this method of concealing the fact. Small technical errors, like the misspelling of a word, should not be noticed if the meaning of the ballot is clear. For instance, if at the trial of a member a ballot was written "gilty," every one knows what was intended. In all cases where the name on the ballot sounds like the name of one of the candidates it should be so credited. If a ballot is written "Johnson," or "Johnston," or "Johnstone," it should be credited to the candidate whose name is one of these: but if there are two candidates with these names and no eligible member with the name on the ballot, it must be rejected as illegal, or reported to the chair, who will at once submit the question to the assembly as to whom the ballot should be credited. If these doubtful ballots will not affect the result, the tellers may make their full report without asking for instructions in regard to them, placing these doubtful votes opposite the exact name as written on the ballot. Votes for ineligible persons and fraudulent votes should be reported under the heading of "Illegal Votes," after the legal votes. When two or three filled-out ballots are folded together they are counted as one fraudulent vote. The names of the candidates should be arranged in order, the one receiving the highest number of legal votes being first. In reporting the number of votes cast and the number necessary for election, all votes except blanks must be counted. Suppose the tellers find 100 ballot papers, 4 of which are blank. 1 contains two filled-out ones folded together, and 50 are cast for a person who is ineligible because of having held the office as long as permitted by the constitution: the tellers' report should be in this form:

Number of votes cast	96
Necessary for election	49
Mr. A received	37
Mr. B received	8

Illegal Votes.

Mr. C (ineligible) received	50
One ballot containing two for Mr. D, folded together, rejected as fraudulent	1

The teller first named, standing, addresses the chair, reads the report and hands it to the chairman, and takes his seat, without saying who is elected. The chairman again reads the report of the tellers and declares who is elected. In the case just given he says there is no election, stating the reason. If no one is elected, it is necessary to ballot again, and to continue balloting until there is an election. The chairman should always vote in case of a ballot. Should he fail to do so before the polls are closed, he cannot then do it without the permission of the assembly. When the tellers report, they should hand the ballots to the secretary, who should retain them until it is certain that the assembly will not order a recount, which is within its power to do by a majority vote.

*Yeas and Nays,** *or Roll Call.* When a vote has been ordered to be taken by yeas and nays [see 25 for the motion] the chair puts the question in a form similar to this: "As many as are in favor of the adoption of these resolutions will, as their names are called, answer *yes* [or *yea*]; those opposed will answer *no* [or *nay*]." The chairman then directs the clerk to call the roll. The negative being put at the same time as the affirmative, it is too late, after one person has answered to the roll call, to renew the debate. The clerk calls the roll, and each member, as his name is called, rises and answers "yes" or "no," or "present" if he does not wish to vote, and the clerk notes the answers in separate columns. Upon the completion of the roll call the clerk reads the names of those who answered in the affirmative, and afterwards those in the negative, and then those who answered "present," that mis-

---

* Taking a vote by yeas and nays, which has the effect to place on the record how each member votes, is peculiar to this country, and, while it consumes a great deal of time, is rarely useful in ordinary societies. While it can never be used to hinder business, as long as the above rule is observed, it should not be used at all in a mass meeting, or in any other assembly whose members are not responsible to a constituency. By the Constitution, one-fifth of the members present can, in either house of Congress, order a vote to be taken by yeas and nays. In representative bodies this method of voting is very useful, especially where the proceedings are published, as it enables the people to know how their representatives voted on important measures. If there is no legal or constitutional provision for the yeas and nays being ordered by a minority in a representative body, they should adopt a rule allowing the yeas and nays to be ordered by a one-fifth vote, as in Congress, or even by a much smaller number. In some small bodies a vote on a resolution must be taken by yeas and nays, upon the demand of a single member.

takes may be corrected; he then gives the number voting on each side to the chairman, who announces the result. An entry must be made in the minutes of the names of all voting in the affirmative, and also of those in the negative, and those who answered "present." A convenient method of noting the answers at the roll call is to write the figure 1 on the left of the name of the first member answering in the affirmative, the figure 2 to the left of the second name in the affirmative, and so on. The negative answers are treated similarly, being entered on the right of the names, and those answering "present" should be entered similarly in a third column. In this way the last figures on each side at any time show how the vote stands at that time. The yeas and nays cannot be ordered in committee of the whole.

General Consent. Business can be expedited greatly by avoiding the formality of motions and voting in routine business and on questions of little importance, the chair assuming general (unanimous) consent until some one objects. It does not necessarily mean that every member is in favor of the motion, but, that knowing it is useless to oppose it, or even to discuss it, the opposition simply acquiesces in the informality. Thus, in the case of approving the minutes, the chair inquires if there are any corrections, and, if one is suggested, it is made: when no correction [or no further correction] is suggested, the chair says: "There being no corrections [or no further corrections] the minutes stand approved." While routine and minor matters can be rapidly disposed of in this way, if at any time objection is made with reasonable promptness, the chair ignores what has been done in that case even if he has announced the result, and requires a regular vote. [See also page 202.]

Absentee Voting. In a strictly deliberative assembly no member can vote who is not present when the question is completely put. But in many societies the membership is scattered all over a state, or even still wider, and it has been found expedient to provide a method of voting that will enable all the members to vote upon certain matters, as upon amendments to constitutions, by-laws, and in elections of officers. This provision, when it is deemed advisable to adopt it, should be placed in the constitution or by-laws, as otherwise, unless the charter or state laws authorize absentee voting, no member can vote except in person. There are two forms of absentee voting—by mail, and proxy voting.

Voting by Mail is used for election of officers, and for amendments to the constitution or by-laws, and for such other important matters as the society may order to be voted on in this way. If an amendment to the by-laws is to be voted on by mail, a printed copy of the proposed amendment is mailed to every member, with the words "yes" and "no" printed underneath, or on a separate slip, with directions to cross out one of them, and return in the enclosed envelope, upon which should be printed the words, "Ballot for Amendment to Constitution." This envelope should usually have the signature of the voter on it, and be sealed and enclosed in another one addressed to the secretary, or to the chairman of the tellers, so that the inner envelope will not be opened except by the tellers when the votes are counted. If it is desired to present the arguments pro and con, the society can allow the leaders on the two sides to prepare brief statements to be printed and mailed with the proposed amendment to every member. Instead of having the voter's signature on the inner envelope, it may be placed on the ballot, but a place for the signature should be indicated, so that there may be some means of protection against votes being cast by other than legal voters. Voting by mail cannot be a secret ballot, as it is necessary for the tellers to know by whom each vote is cast. By some such method as the above it is practicable to give all the members, however scattered they may be, an opportunity to vote on questions of great importance.

Proxy Voting. A proxy is a power of attorney given by one person to another to vote in his stead, and it is also used to designate the person who holds the power of attorney. It is unknown to a strictly deliberative assembly, and is in conflict with the idea of the equality of members, which is a fundamental principle of deliberative assemblies. There can be but little use for debate where one member has more votes than another, possibly more than all the others combined. If the proxy voting is limited to the election of a board of directors, as it is practically in stock corporations, and if, also, the proxies must be given to members of the corporation in all cases where it requires an election to become a member—with these two limitations proxy voting would be useful and do no harm. In stock companies the members meet only annually to elect directors, who elect the officers and transact the business of the corporation. Though the directors are elected largely by proxies, their own meetings, where all the business is done, are as secret as they choose to make them, no proxies being allowed in them, and therefore proxy voting does not interfere with their business. As any one can dispose of his stock to any one else, there is no objection to his appointing any one as his proxy. But the case is very different with many incorporated societies of a social, benevolent, or religious character, whose business meetings are sometimes secret. Their membership cannot be transferred by the members like stock, and therefore they should not be allowed to appoint any proxies who are not members of the organization. The state law is above the by-laws of the society, and if the state law empowers members of all corporations to appoint proxies to vote at all business meetings, no by-laws of an incorporated secret society could prevent non-members holding proxies from attending and voting at all business meetings of the society. This should not be the case. With stock corporations it does no harm, because all the business is done by directors, and no proxies are allowed in their meetings, and no one can be present without their consent. But in many societies of the kind mentioned the business is transacted in meetings attended by none but members, and unlimited proxies would be a serious interference with their work. If the state law requires proxy voting in all corporations, it should be limited to the election of officers, including directors, and also the proxies should be required to be held by members of the corporation in all organizations whose primary object is not pecuniary profit.

47. Votes that are Null and Void even if Unanimous. No motion is in order that conflicts with the laws of the nation, or state, or with the assembly's constitution or by-laws, and if such a motion is adopted, even by a unanimous vote, it is null and void. No rule that conflicts with a rule of a higher order is of any authority; thus, a by-law providing for the suspension by general consent of an article of the constitution would be null and void; so, the general parliamentary rule allowing a two-thirds vote to amend the by-laws after due notice, is only in force when the by-laws are silent on the subject. Rules that protect absentees cannot be suspended informally by general consent, or formally by a unanimous vote, as the absentees have not given their consent. For instance, a rule requiring the giving of a specified notice of certain motions, as an amendment of the by-laws, cannot be suspended by general consent or by a unanimous vote. When a vote is required to be taken by ballot, the object is to enable members to conceal their votes, and any motion that defeats this object is out of order. Thus, when the rules require the vote to be by ballot, as is usual in elections to office or membership, this rule cannot be suspended even by general consent, because no one can object without exposing his vote, which he cannot be compelled to do. When the election must be by ballot, a motion to have the ballot cast by one person is out of order. So, when the rules require the vote to be by ballot, a motion to make unanimous a vote that was not unanimous, must be voted on by ballot, as otherwise the vote would not be secret.

48. Motions requiring more than a Majority Vote. *Majority Vote.* Any legitimate motion not included among those mentioned below as requiring more than a majority vote, requires for its adoption only a majority; that is, more than half of the votes cast, ignoring blanks, at a legal meeting where a quorum is present, unless a larger vote for its adoption is required by the rules of the assembly.

General Consent or Unanimous Vote. By general, or unanimous, or silent, consent the assembly can do business with little regard for the rules of procedure, as they are made for the protection of the minority, and when there is no minority to protect, there is little use for the restraint of the rules, except such as protect the rights of absent members, or the right to a secret vote. In the former case the consent of the absentees cannot be given, and in the latter case the consent cannot be withheld by the minority without exposing their votes, which they cannot be compelled to do. When the election is not by ballot and there are several candidates one of whom receives a majority vote, sometimes a motion is made to make the vote unanimous. It should never be made except by the candidate with the largest number of votes after the successful one, or his representative, and even then its propriety is doubtful. One negative vote defeats a motion to make a vote unanimous, as a single objection defeats a request for general consent.

By the legitimate use of the principle that the rules are designed for the protection of the minority, and generally need not be strictly enforced when there is no minority to protect, business may be greatly expedited. When there is evidently no opposition, the formality of voting can be avoided by the chair's asking if there is any objection to the proposed action, and if there is none, announcing the result. The action thus taken is said to be done by general consent, or unanimous or silent consent. Thus, after an order has been adopted limiting the speeches to two minutes each, if a speaker is so interesting that when his time has expired there is a general demand for him to go on, the chair, instead of waiting for a motion and taking a vote, could accept it as the will of the assembly that the speaker's time be extended, and would direct him to proceed. Or, he might say that if there is no objection the member's time will be extended two minutes, or some other time. [See also page 198.]

Two-thirds Vote. A two-thirds vote means two-thirds of the votes cast, ignoring blanks which should never be counted. This must not be confused with a vote of two-thirds of the members present, or two-thirds of the members, terms sometimes used in by-laws. To illustrate the difference: Suppose 14 members vote on a question in a meeting of a society where 20 are present out of a total membership of 70, a two-thirds vote would be 10; a two-thirds vote of the members present would be 14; and a vote of two-thirds of the members would be 47.

There has been established as a compromise between the rights of the individual and the rights of the assembly the principle that a two-thirds vote is required to adopt any motion that suspends or modifies a rule of order previously adopted; or prevents the introduction of a question for consideration; or closes, or limits, or extends the limits of debate; or limits the freedom of nomination or voting; or closes nominations or the polls; or deprives one of membership or office. It will be found that every motion in the following list belongs to one of the classes just mentioned.

Motions Requiring a Two-thirds Vote.*

Amend (Annul, Repeal, or Rescind) any part of the Constitution, By-laws, or Rules of Order, previously adopted; it also requires previous notice **68**

Amend or Rescind a Standing Rule, a Program or Order of Business, or a Resolution, previously adopted, without notice being given at a previous meeting or in the call for the meeting **37**

Take up a Question out of its Proper Order **22**

Suspend the Rules **22**

Make a Special Order **20**

Discharge an Order of the Day before it is pending **20**

Refuse to Proceed to the Orders of the Day **20**

Sustain an Objection to the Consideration of a Question **23**

Previous Question **29**

Limit, or Extend the Limits, of Debate **30**

---

* The U. S. Constitution requires a two-thirds vote of both Houses to pass a resolution proposing an amendment to the Constitution, to pass a vetoed bill, or to remove political disabilities; a two-thirds vote of either House to expel a member; and a vote of two-thirds of the Senators present to ratify a treaty or convict on an impeachment. The House requires a two-thirds vote to suspend the rules, but is obliged to allow a majority to order the previous question or to limit debate, as otherwise its business could never be transacted. Still, a bill cannot be passed without at least forty minutes of debate, as that is allowed after the suspension of the rules or the previous question has been ordered. **[See foot note to 44.]**

Art. IX. Committees and Boards

49. **Committees Classified.** A Committee is a body of one or more persons appointed or elected by an assembly or society to consider, or investigate, or take action in regard to, certain matters or subjects, or to do all of these things. Committees may be divided into two distinct classes:

(1) Boards of Managers or Directors, Boards of Trustees, Executive Committees, etc.

(2) Ordinary Committees, Special or

Standing, and Committee of the Whole and its substitutes.

These different kinds of committees are considered separately in the following five sections.

50. Boards of Managers or Directors, Boards of Trustees, Executive Committees, etc. Committees of this class are essentially small deliberative assemblies, subordinate to the body that appoints them, with their duties and authority, and the number of their regular meetings and their quorums, defined by the parent body, or by its authority. Boards or Committees of this class are usually appointed by organizations that meet only annually or quarterly. With such an organization it is customary and necessary to delegate to a committee, usually known as the Board of Managers or Directors, all its authority, with slight limitations, to be exercised between its meetings. The by-laws of the Board are adopted by the parent body, or the Board may be authorized to adopt its own by-laws. It is usual to authorize the Board to appoint from its membership an Executive Committee of a specified number who shall have all the power of the Board between the meetings of the Board, just as the Board has all the power of the Society between the meetings of the Society, except that the subordinate body cannot modify any action taken by its superior. The Executive Committee should be small and the members should live near enough each other to be able to have frequent regular meetings, besides special meetings in emergencies. Where the organization is local, such as a society for sustaining an orphan asylum, the Board of Managers usually divides itself into committees having charge of different branches of the work during the intervals between the monthly or quarterly meetings of the Board, when these committees report on the work done. It is seldom that resolutions or other matters are referred to boards or committees of this class for them to report back to the society with recommendations. If papers are referred to them it is usually for their information and action. They are organized as any other deliberative assembly with a chairman and a secretary, whom they elect if they are not appointed by the society. Frequently the by-laws of the society make its president and its corresponding, or executive secretary, ex-officio, [51] president and secretary of the Board of Managers.

In large boards business is transacted the same as in the society meetings; but in small boards the same formality is not necessary or usual, the informality observed by committees being generally allowed. In a board meeting where there are not more than about a dozen present, for instance, it is not necessary to rise in order to make a motion, nor to wait for recognition by the chair before speaking or making a motion, nor for a motion to have a second; nor is there any limit to the number of speeches, nor does the chairman leave the chair when making a motion or discussing a question. The formalities necessary in order to transact business in a large assembly would hinder business in so small a body.

Boards are often constituted so that the term of office of, say, one-third of its members expires each year. After each annual meeting in such case, the board elects new officers and committees, the same as if the entire board had been re-elected. All unfinished business falls to the ground when the new board is elected.

It is customary for the by-laws to require an annual report from the Board of Managers, which usually gives a brief account of its doings for the year with recommendations for the future. After discussion, and amendment if necessary, the report is usually adopted by the society and published in its annual proceedings as the report of the board. In such a case, care should be taken in publishing it to inclose in brackets all that has been struck out, and to put in italics whatever has been inserted, and to insert a note to that effect at the beginning of the report, so that exactly what the board recommended can readily be seen. The minutes should read thus: "The Board of Managers submitted its report which after discussion and amendment was adopted as follows, the words in brackets having been struck out and those underscored (in italics) having been inserted before the report was adopted." The society cannot alter the report of the board. It may decline to indorse it, or even to allow it to be printed, but it cannot make it appear that the board stated anything different from what it has reported. By the above plan is shown exactly what the board reported and what the society adopted, or endorsed.

51. Ex-Officio Members of Boards and Committees. Frequently boards and committees contain some members who are members by virtue of their office, and, therefore, are termed ex-officio members. When such a member ceases to hold the office his membership of the board terminates automatically. If the ex-officio member is under the control of the society, there is no distinction between him and the other members except where the president is ex-officio member of all committees, in which case it is evidently the intention to permit, not to require, him to act as a member of the various committees, and therefore in counting a quorum he should not be counted as a member. The president is not a member of any committee except by virtue of a special rule, unless he is so appointed by the assembly. If the ex-officio member is not under the authority of the society, he has all the privileges, including the right to vote, but none of the obligations of membership; as when the governor of a state is, ex-officio, a manager or a trustee of a private academy.

52. **Committees, Special and Standing.** It is usual in deliberative assemblies, to have all preliminary work in the preparation of matter for their action done by means of committees. The committee may be either a "standing committee," appointed for a definite time, as a session or a year; or a "special [or select] committee," appointed for a special purpose; or a "committee of the whole" consisting of the entire assembly. [For method of appointing committees of the whole, see **55**; other committees, see Commit, **32**.] Committees of the whole are not used much except in legislative bodies, and when the word committees is used in this Manual, unless specified to the contrary, standing or special committees are meant. Unless the assembly has appointed a chairman, either directly or through its presiding officer, the first named on a committee, and in his absence the next named member, becomes chairman, and so on and should act as such unless the committee by a majority of its number elects a chairman, which it has the right to do if the assembly has not appointed one, and which a standing committee usually does. The clerk should furnish him, or, in his absence, some other member of the committee, with notice of the appointment of the committee, the names of the members, the

papers or matter referred to it, and such instructions as the assembly has decided upon. Upon the committee's request, all papers and books necessary for the proper performance of its duties should be turned over to it by the proper officers.

It is the duty of the chairman to call the committee together, but, if he is absent, or neglects or declines to call a meeting of the committee, it is the duty of the committee to meet on the call of any two of its members. In small special committees the chairman usually acts as secretary, but in large ones and in all standing committees, it is customary to elect a secretary, who keeps a brief memorandum of what is done, for the use of the committee. Members of the society have a right to appear at the committee meetings and present their views on the subject before it at such reasonable times as, upon request, the committee may appoint. But during the deliberations of the committee no one has a right to be present, except members of the committee.

The rules of the assembly, as far as possible, apply to the committee, but motions to close or limit debate are not allowed, and there is no limit to the number of times a member may speak, and unless the committee is very large, it is not necessary for any one to rise and address the chair before making a motion or speaking, nor does the chairman rise to put the question, nor does he leave the chair to speak or make motions, nor are motions seconded. These formalities are unnecessary because the committee is so small, but, unless agreed to by general consent, all questions must be put to vote. Instead of the chairman's abstaining from speaking on questions, he is, usually, the most active participant in the discussions and work of the committee. In order that the assembly may have the benefit of the matured judgment of the committee, a reconsideration of a vote must be allowed regardless of the time and of previous reconsideration, and it may be moved by any one who did not vote with the minority, even if he was absent when the previous vote was taken; but it shall require a two-thirds vote for its adoption unless every member who voted with the majority is either present or received ample notice of the meeting and that the reconsideration was to be moved. This prevents taking advantage of the absence of members to reverse action, and enables members who were absent to bring up the question of reconsideration.

The committee constitute a miniature assembly, being able to act only when a quorum (a majority of the members) is present. If a paper is referred to them, they must not write on it, but should write their amendments on a separate sheet. If the amendments are numerous it is better to write out a substitute and submit it. If a resolution is referred to a committee while a motion to postpone indefinitely is pending, only the resolution is referred to the committee, the motion to postpone indefinitely being ignored. If amendments are pending they go to the committee, who may recommend their adoption or rejection, or make no recommendation in regard to them. If the committee originate the paper, all amendments must be incorporated in it. When they originate it, usually one member has previously prepared a draft, which is read entirely through, and then read by paragraphs, the chairman pausing after each paragraph, and asking: "Are there any amendments proposed to this paragraph?" No vote is taken on the adoption of the separate paragraphs; but, after the whole paper has been read in this way, it is open to amendment generally, by striking out any paragraph, or by substituting or inserting new ones, or by substituting an entirely new paper for it. If there is a preamble it is considered last. When the entire paper has been amended to suit the committee, they should adopt it as their report, and direct the chairman or some other member to report it to the assembly. When committees are appointed to investigate, or to report upon, certain matters, the report should close with, or be accompanied by, formal resolutions covering all recommendations, so that when their report is made no motion is necessary except to adopt the resolutions.

If the report is written in this form, "Your committee are of the opinion that Mr. A's bill should be paid," there might be some doubt as to the effect of the adoption of the recommendation or the report. The report should close with a recommendation that the following order be adopted: "Ordered, That the Treasurer pay Mr. A's bill for $10.15." If a report recommends that charges be preferred against Mr. B, it should close with recommending the adoption of resolutions, which should be written out, providing for holding an adjourned meeting, and for citing the member to appear at the adjourned meeting for trial on charges that must be specified. These should be prepared by the committee and submitted as a part of their report. The committee should never leave to others the responsibility of preparing resolutions to carry out their recommendations. They should consider this as one of their most important duties.

When the report has been adopted by the committee a clear copy is made, usually commencing in a style similar to this: "The committee to whom was referred (state the matter referred), beg leave to submit the following report;" or, "Your committee appointed to (specify the object), respectfully report," etc. If the report is of much importance it should be signed by all the members concurring in the report; but when it is of little importance, or merely recommends amendments, etc., it may be signed by the chairman alone, his signature being followed by the word "Chairman." He should not, however, place "Chairman" after his signature except when he signs the report alone and by the authority of the committee. The report must always be in the third person though written and signed by only one.

The signature may be preceded by the words, "Respectfully submitted," but it is not necessary. Usually the report is not dated or addressed, and sometimes it consists merely of a resolution, or a set of resolutions. In the latter case the chairman states he is instructed by the committee to submit and to move the adoption of the resolutions. The report of the majority is the report of the committee and should never be referred to as the majority report.

If the minority submit a report, (or more properly, their "views,") it may commence thus: "The undersigned, a minority of the committee appointed, etc., not agreeing with the majority, desire to express their views in the case." After the committee's report has been read and the motion to adopt has been made and the question stated, it is usual to allow the minority to present their views, but if any one objects to its reception the chair should put the question to vote on its being received. It requires a majority vote to receive it, the question being undebatable. When the minority report is read it is for information, and it cannot be acted upon except by a motion to substitute it for the report of the committee. Whether the views of the minority are read or not, any one can move to substitute the resolutions they recommend for those recommended by the committee. Where the minority cannot agree, each member may submit his views separately. In some cases a member agrees to the report with a single exception, in which case instead of submitting his views separately, after all have signed who agree to the report he may write that he agrees to the report except the part which he specifies, and then sign the statement.

The committee's report* can contain only that which has been agreed to by a majority vote at a meeting of which every member has been notified, or at an adjourned meeting thereof (a quorum, a majority of the members, being present), except where it is impracticable to have a meeting of the committee, when it may contain what is agreed to by every member. If a committee is appointed from different sections of the country with the expectation that its work will be done by correspondence, its report can contain only what is agreed to by a majority of the members.

A committee, except a committee of the whole, can appoint a sub-committee which, however, reports to the committee, and never to the assembly. This sub-committee must consist of members of the committee, except in cases where the committee is appointed to take action that requires the assistance of

---

* In Congress nothing can be "the report of the committee but what has been agreed to in committee actually assembled," so that a report signed by a majority of a committee acting separately was ruled out. In some societies, however, it is often impracticable to have regular committee meetings with a majority present.

others, as to make arrangements for holding a bazaar. In such a case it is best to appoint the committee with power to appoint such subcommittees as are required; or, as is frequently done, to appoint the committee "with power," which means with power to take all the steps necessary to carry out its instructions. A committee has no power to punish its members for disorderly conduct, its recourse being to report the facts to the assembly. No allusion can be made in the assembly to what has occurred during the deliberations of the committee, unless it is by a report of the committee or by general consent. When a special committee is through with the business assigned it, a motion is made for the committee to "rise" (which is equivalent to the motion to adjourn without day), and that the chairman (or some member who is more familiar with the subject) make its report to the assembly. A special committee ceases to exist as soon as the assembly receives its report. When a committee adjourns without appointing a time for the next meeting, it is considered as having adjourned at the call of the chair, so that all the meetings of a special committee constitute one session. A meeting of a special committee may be called at any time by the chairman or by any two of its members, every member being notified. When a committee adjourns to meet at another time, it is not necessary (though usually advisable) that absent members should be notified of the adjourned meeting.

A standing committee is either wholly, or partially, elected at each annual meeting in ordinary societies, and immediately thereafter it reorganizes by electing a chairman (unless he has been appointed by the assembly) and a secretary. Therefore, a standing committee must report at the annual meeting, or before, on everything referred to it during the year. The motion to rise is never used in standing committees or boards, nor is it used in other committees except when the committee is ready to report so that it will never meet again. A special committee is appointed for a specific purpose, and until the duty assigned it by the society is accomplished it continues to exist, unless sooner discharged, which requires a two-thirds vote if done without notice being given. The fact that an annual meeting has intervened does not discharge a special committee appointed by a society. But in an elected or appointed body, as a convention, special committees that have not reported cease to exist when the new officers assume their duties at the next annual meeting. When discharged, the chairman of the committee returns to the secretary all documents received from him.

While in small assemblies, especially in those where but little business is done, there is not much need of committees, in large assemblies, or in those doing a great deal of business, committees are of the utmost importance. When a committee is properly selected, in nine cases out of ten its action decides that of the assembly. A committee for *action* should be small, and consist only of those heartily in favor of the proposed action. If one not in sympathy with it is appointed, he should ask to be excused. A committee for deliberation or investigation, on the contrary, should be large, and represent all parties in the assembly, so that its opinion will carry with it as great weight as possible. The usefulness of the committee will be greatly impaired if any important faction of the assembly is unrepresented on the committee. The appointment of a committee is fully explained in **32**.

53. Reception of Reports. When there is a place in the order of business provided for reports of committees, they are not made until they are called for by the chair. Upon the arrival of the time for these reports, the chair calls for the reports of such officers and standing committees as are required to make reports, in the order in which they are arranged in the rules; after which he calls for the reports of the special committees in the order of their appointment. When called upon, the reporting member (who is the chairman of the committee unless another member is appointed to make the report) rises and addresses the chair, and, when recognized, reads the report and hands it to the presiding officer, or the secretary, and, when necessary, moves its adoption or acceptance as explained in the next section. If the committee reports back a paper with amendments, the amendments are read with sufficient of the related parts to make them understood. If it is desired to have a report made earlier than the rules allow, it can be done, by a two-thirds vote, by suspending the rules [22] and receiving the report at once.

If the order of business makes no provision for the report of the committee, the reporting member, when ready to report, obtains the floor when no business is pending, and informs the assembly that the committee to which was referred such a subject or paper has agreed upon a report which he is now prepared to submit. If the chair thinks the assembly wishes to hear the report he directs him to proceed, whereupon he reads the report and hands it to the chairman and makes the proper motion for its disposal. If before it is read any one objects to its reception, or if the chair is in doubt as to whether it should be received now, he puts to the assembly the question, "Shall the report be received now?" It requires a majority vote to receive it, and the question is undebatable. If the vote is in the negative, a time for the reception of the report should be appointed either by a vote or by general consent. Usually no motions are made or votes taken in regard to receiving reports, these matters being all settled informally by general consent.

If the report is a final one, when the assembly has received the report the committee has completed its work, and, without any motion, it is automatically discharged from further consideration of the subject, and, if it is a special committee, it ceases to exist. If the report is only a partial one the committee is not discharged unless the assembly so votes. If the subject is recommitted the committee is revived (unless the reference is to another committee), and all parts of the report that have not been adopted by the assembly are ignored by the committee as if the report had never been made. If any member or members wish to submit the views of the minority it is customary to receive such a report immediately after receiving the report of the committee. In such case the reporting member should notify the assembly that the views of the minority will be submitted in a separate paper. As soon as the chair has stated the question on the report, he should call for the views of the minority, which are then read for information. They cannot be acted upon unless it is moved to substitute them for the committee's report, or rather to substitute the recommendations of the minority for those of the committee.

A very common error is, after a report has been read, to move that it be received, whereas the fact that it has been read shows that it has been already received by the assembly. Another mistake, less common, but dangerous, is to vote that the report be accepted, which is equivalent to adopting it [see next section], when the intention is only to have the report up for consideration and afterwards to vote on its adoption.

54. Adoption or Acceptance of Reports. When the report of a committee has been received, that is, has been presented to the assembly and either read or handed to the chair or the secretary, the next business in order is the disposal of the report, the proper disposition depending upon its nature.

(1) If the report contains only a statement of fact or opinion for the information of the assembly, the reporting member makes no motion for its disposal, as there is no necessity for action on the report. But if any action is taken, the proper motion, which should be made by some one else, is to "accept the report," which has the effect of endorsing the statement and making the assembly assume responsibility for it.

If it is a financial report, as in case of a board of trustees or a treasurer, it should be referred to an auditing committee, as the vote to accept the report does not endorse the accuracy of the figures, for the assembly can only be sure of that by having the report audited. Whenever such a financial report is made, the chair, without any motion, should say it is referred to the auditing committee or auditors, if there are any. If there are none, then the proper motion is to refer it to an auditing committee to be appointed by the chair. When the auditing committee reports, this report should be accepted, or adopted, which carries with it the endorsement of the financial report.

(2) If the report contains recommendations not in the form of motions, they should all be placed at the end of the report, even if they have been given separately before, and the proper motion is to adopt the recommendations.

(3) If the report concludes with a resolution or a series of resolutions, the proper course is for the reporting member to move that the resolution or resolutions be adopted or agreed to. This method should be adopted whenever practicable.

(4) If a committee reports back a resolution which was referred to it, the motion to postpone indefinitely, if it was pending, is ignored; if an amendment was pending it should be reported on. The form of the question to be stated by the chair depends upon the recommendation of the committee as follows: (*a*) If the committee recommends its adoption, or makes no recommendation (where it can come to no agreement), the question should be stated on the amendment if there was one pending, and then on the reso-

lution. These motions were pending when the question was referred to the committee, and therefore should not be made again. (*b*) If the recommendation is that the resolution be not adopted, the question on the resolution, when it is put, should be stated thus: "The question is on the adoption of the resolution, the recommendation of the committee to the contrary notwithstanding." A similar course is pursued if the committee recommends that an amendment be not adopted. (*c*) If the committee recommends that the resolution be postponed indefinitely, or postponed to a certain time, the question should be on the postponement, and, if that is lost, then on the resolution.

(*d*) If the committee reports back a resolution or paper with amendments, the reporting member reads only the amendments with sufficient of the context to make them understood and then moves their adoption. The chairman, after stating the question on the adoption of the amendments, calls for the reading of the first amendment, after which it is open for debate and amendment. A vote is then taken on adopting this amendment, and the next is read, and so on till the amendments are adopted or rejected, admitting amendments to the committee's amendments, but no others. When through with the committee's amendments, the chairman pauses for any other amendments to be proposed by the assembly;

and when these are voted on he puts the question on agreeing to, or adopting, the paper as amended, unless, in a case like revising the by-laws, they have been already adopted. By suspending the rules [22], or by general consent, a report can be at once adopted without following any of the above routine.

If the amendments do not call for debate or amendment, as when reported from the committee of the whole, where they have been already discussed, the chair puts a single question on all the committee's amendments except those for which a member asks a separate vote, thus: "As many as are in favor of adopting the amendments recommended by the committee, except those for which a separate vote has been asked, say *aye;* those opposed say *no.*" He then takes up the remaining amendments separately in their order.

(*e*) If the committee reports back a resolution with a substitute which it recommends for adoption, the chair states the question on the substitute, if there were no amendments pending when the resolution was committed. If, however, amendments were pending when the resolution was committed, the chair first states the questions on those pending amendments, and when they are disposed of he states the question on the substitute. In either case the substitute is treated like any other substitute motion, the resolution being first perfected by amendments and then the substitute resolution. After both have been thus perfected the question is put on the substitution, and finally on the resolution. If the substitute is lost the resolution is open to amendments proposed by members. (*f*) If the report is of a nomination committee no vote should be taken, any more than if a member had made the nominations. (*g*) If the report is from the membership committee, the chair at once states the question on the reception as members of the candidates recommended by the committee.

A partial report of a committee is treated the same as the final report. If it reports progress only, without recommendations or conclusions, it is treated as any other report for information, and no action need be taken. But, if the partial report recommends action, then the question is to be put on adopting the report, or its recommendations, or the resolutions, the same as if it were the final report.

While it is customary in ordinary societies to make and second a motion to accept or adopt a committee's report, yet if the motion is not made and the chair deems it best to have a vote taken on the question, he may state the appropriate question without waiting for a motion, accepting the submission of the report by a committee as equivalent to moving the adoption of the appropriate motion for disposing of it, just as is the case when one offers a resolution. To wait to see if two members are in favor of a proposition which at least two have signed, or authorized the chairman, or reporting member, to sign, would appear useless. In ordinary societies the chairman of the assembly usually knows better than the reporting member how the business should be managed, especially if a resolution is reported with many amendments. However, unless the assembly is accustomed to having its chairman put the proper questions on the report without any formal motion, it is better for the reporting member to move the "adoption" of the resolutions or recommendations, as that is generally understood.

When the chair has stated the question on the adoption of the recommendations or resolutions, or of the report, the matter under consideration is open to debate and amendment, and may have applied to it any of the subsidiary motions, like other main questions. Its consideration cannot be objected to if the matter was referred to the committee. While the report of the committee or its resolutions may be amended by the assembly, these amendments only affect that which the assembly adopts, as the assembly cannot in any way change the committee's report.

For example: A committee expresses the opinion that Mr. A has no right to commit a certain act, and the assembly strikes out this statement from the report before adopting it. This does not alter the report, but, when the assembly adopts the report, this statement is not adopted. So with a recommendation or a resolution: the assembly may strike out or add one or more recommendations or resolutions before adopting, but that does not alter the committee's report. If the proceedings are published, the committee's report should be printed exactly as it was submitted with the amendments printed below; or, still better, all words struck out should be enclosed in brackets and all words inserted should be printed in italics. and a note to that effect inserted at the beginning.

While the motions to adopt, to accept, etc., are often used indiscriminately, and the adoption of any one of them has the effect of endorsing or adopting the opinions, actions, recommendations, or resolutions submitted by the committee, as the case may be, yet it is better to use them as heretofore stated. If only one term is used, the word "adopt" is preferable, as it is least liable to be misunderstood.

55. Committee of the Whole. When an assembly has to consider a subject which it does not wish to refer to a committee, and yet where the subject matter is not well digested and put into proper form for its definite action, or when, for any other reason, it is desirable for the assembly to consider a subject with all the freedom of an ordinary committee, it is the practice to refer the matter to the "Committee of the Whole." If it is desired to consider the question at once, the motion is made, "That the assembly do now resolve itself into a committee of the whole, to take under consideration," etc., or, "That we go into committee of the whole to consider," etc., specifying the subject. This is really a motion to "commit." [See 32 for its order of precedence, etc.] If adopted, the chairman immediately calls another member to the chair, and takes his place as a member of the committee. The committee is under the rules of the assembly, excepting as stated hereafter in this section.

The only motions in order are to amend and adopt, and that the committee "rise and report," as it cannot adjourn; nor can it order the "yeas and nays." An appeal from the decision of the chair can be made, and it must be voted on directly, as it cannot be laid on the table or postponed, those motions not being allowed in committee of the whole. Each member can speak only once on the appeal. The only way to close or limit debate in committee of the whole is for the assembly, before going into committee of the whole, to vote that the debate in committee shall cease at a certain time, or that after a certain time no debate shall be allowed, excepting on new amendments, and then only one speech in favor of and one against it, of, say, five minutes each; or in some other way to regulate the time for debate.

If no limit is prescribed, any member may speak as often as he can get the floor, and as long each time as is allowed in debate in the assembly, but he cannot speak a second time provided a member wishes the floor who has not spoken on that particular question. Debate having been closed at a particular time by order of the assembly, the committee has not the power, even by unanimous consent, to extend the time. The committee cannot refer the subject to another committee. Like other committees, it cannot alter the text of any resolution referred to it; but if the resolution originated in the committee, then all the amendments are incorporated in it.

When the committee is through with the consideration of the subject referred to it, or if it wishes to adjourn, or to have the assembly limit debate, a motion is made that "the committee rise and report," etc., specifying the result of its proceedings. The motion to "rise" is equivalent to the motion to adjourn in the assembly, and is always in order (except while voting or when another member has the floor), and is undebatable and cannot be amended. As soon as this motion is adopted the presiding officer takes the chair, and the chairman of the committee, having resumed his place in the assembly, rises, addresses the chair, and says: "The Committee of the Whole has had under consideration (here he describes the resolution or other matter) and has directed me to report the same with (or without, as the case may be) amendments," provided the committee has concluded its business. If the committee has failed to come to a conclusion, strike out of the report all after "and has" and insert "come to no conclusion thereon." If no amendments are reported, the chair at once states the question on the resolution or other matter referred to the committee. If amendments are reported the reporting member reads them, and hands the paper to the chair, who reads, and states and puts the question on the amendments as a whole, unless a member asks for a separate vote on one or more amendments, in which case a single vote is taken on all the other amendments, and then the question is stated separately on each of the amendments for which a separate vote was asked. The amendments may be debated and amended.

The secretary does not record in the minutes the proceedings of the committee, but should keep a memorandum of the proceedings for its use. In large assemblies the secretary vacates his chair, which is occupied by the chairman of the committee, and the assistant secretary acts as secretary of the committee. Should the committee become disorderly, and the chairman be unable to control it, the presiding officer should take the chair and declare the committee dissolved. The quorum of the committee of the whole is the same as that of the assembly [64]. If the committee finds itself without a quorum, it can only rise and report the fact to the assembly, which in such case must adjourn.

In large assemblies, such as the U. S. House of Representatives, where a member can speak to any question only once, the committee of the whole seems almost a necessity, as it allows the freest discussion of a subject, while at any time it can rise and thus bring into force the strict rules of the assembly. In small assemblies it is usually more convenient to substitute for it either the "Quasi (as if in) Committee of the Whole," as used in the U. S. Senate, or "Informal Consideration," as frequently used in ordinary societies. These are explained in the next two sections.

56. As if in (or Quasi) Committee of the Whole is used in the U. S. Senate instead of the committee of the whole, and is more convenient in small assemblies. The motion should be made in a form similar to this: "I move that the resolution be considered as if in committee of the whole." This being adopted, the question is open to debate and amendment with all the freedom of the committee of the whole. The presiding officer, however, retains the chair, instead of appointing a chairman as is done when the assembly goes into committee of the whole. If any motion is adopted, except an amendment, it puts an end to the quasi committee of the whole. Thus, the motion to commit is equivalent to the following motions when in committee of the whole: (1) That the committee rise; (2) that the committee of the whole be discharged from the further consideration of the subject; and (3) that it be referred to a committee. When the assembly has finished amending the proposition under consideration, without further motion the chairman announces that, "The assembly, acting as if in committee of the whole, has had such subject under consideration, and has made certain amendments," which he then reports. The subject comes before the assembly then as if reported by a committee, the chair stating the question on the amendments as described at the close of the previous section under committee of the whole. The secretary should keep a memorandum of the proceedings while acting as if in committee of the whole, but it should not be entered in the minutes, being only for temporary use. The chairman's report to the assembly should be entered in the minutes, as it belongs to the assembly's proceedings.

57. **Informal Consideration.** In ordinary societies the meetings of which are not large, instead of going into committee of the whole, or considering questions as if in committee of the whole, it is more usual to consider the question informally. The motion is made thus: "I move that the question be considered informally." The effect of the adoption

of this motion is to open the main question and any amendments that may be proposed, to free debate as if in committee of the whole. No member can speak the second time to the same question as long as a member who has not spoken desires the floor. This informal consideration applies only to the main question and its amendments, so that any other motion that is made is under the regular rules of debate. While considering a question informally the assembly by a two-thirds vote may limit the number or length of speeches, or in any other way limit or close the debate. While the consideration of the main question and its amendments is informal, all votes are formal, the informality applying only to the number of speeches allowed in debate. The instant the main question is disposed of temporarily, or permanently, the informal consideration automatically ceases without any motion or vote.

If the question is considered in either the regular committee of the whole or the quasi committee of the whole, it is necessary formally to report the action to the assembly and then take action on the report. Thus, it will be seen that informal consideration is much simpler than either of the methods described in the previous two sections. It can be used to advantage in assemblies that are not very large, instead of the committee of the whole. While this is not a motion to commit, yet it is used for practically the same purpose as the committee of the whole. It ranks just below the motion "to consider as if in committee of the whole," which is just below "to go into committee of the whole."

Art. X. The Officers and the Minutes.

58. Chairman or President. The presiding officer, when no special title has been assigned him, is ordinarily called the Chairman, or the President, or, especially in religious assemblies, the Moderator. In organized societies the constitution always prescribes his title, that of President being most common. In debate he is referred to by his official title and is addressed by prefixing Mr. or Madam, as the case may be, to that title. In referring to himself he should never use the personal pronoun; he generally says, "the chair," which means the presiding officer of the assembly, regardless of whether his position is permanent or temporary. If his position is only temporary he is called the chairman.

His duties are generally as follows: To open the session at the time at which the assembly is to meet, by taking the chair and calling the members to order; to announce the business before the assembly in the order in which it is to be acted upon [65]; to recognize members entitled to the floor [3]; to state [6] and to put to vote [9] all questions which are regularly moved, or necessarily arise in the course of the proceedings, and to announce the result of the vote; to protect the assembly from annoyance from evidently frivolous or dilatory motions by refusing to recognize them [40]; to assist in the expediting of business in every way compatible with the rights of the members, as by allowing brief remarks when undebatable motions are pending, if he thinks it advisable; to restrain the members when engaged in debate, within the rules of order; to enforce on all occasions the observance of order and decorum among the members, deciding all questions of order (subject to an appeal to the assembly by any two members) unless when in doubt he prefers to submit the question for the decision of the assembly [21]; to inform the assembly, when necessary, or when referred to for the purpose, on a point of order or practice pertinent to pending business; to authenticate, by his signature, when necessary, all the acts, orders, and proceedings of the assembly declaring its will and in all things obeying its commands.

In case of fire, riot, or very serious disorder, or other great emergency, the chair has the right and the duty to declare the assembly adjourned to some other time (and place if necessary), if it is impracticable to take a vote, or in his opinion, dangerous to delay for a vote.

The chairman should rise to put a question

to vote, except in very small assemblies, such as boards or committees, but may state it sitting; he should also rise from his seat (without calling any one to the chair) when giving his reasons for his decision upon a point of order, or when speaking upon an appeal, which he can do in preference to other members. During debate he should be seated and pay attention to the speaker, who is required to address his remarks to the presiding officer. He should always refer to himself as "the chair," thus, "The chair decides," etc., not "I decide," etc. When a member has the floor, the chairman cannot interrupt him excepting as provided in 3, so long as he does not transgress any of the rules of the assembly.

If a member of the assembly, he is entitled to vote when the vote is by ballot (but not after the tellers have commenced to count the ballots), and in all other cases where the vote would change the result. Thus, in a case where a two-thirds vote is necessary, and his vote thrown with the minority would prevent the adoption of the question, he can cast his vote; so, also, he can vote with the minority when it will produce a tie vote and thus cause the motion to fail; but he cannot vote twice, first to make a tie, and then to give the casting vote. Whenever a motion is made referring to the chairman only, or which compliments or condemns him with others, it should be put to vote by the Vice President if in the room, or by the Secretary, or on their failure to do so, by the maker of the motion. The chair should not hesitate to put the question on a motion to appoint delegates or a committee on account of his being included.

The chairman cannot close debate unless by order of the assembly, which requires a two-thirds vote; nor can he prevent the making of legitimate motions by hurrying through the proceedings. If members are reasonably prompt in exercising their right to speak or make motions, the chair cannot prevent their doing so. If he has hurriedly taken and announced a vote while a member is rising to address the chair, the vote is null and void, and the member must be recognized. On the other hand the chairman should not permit the object of a meeting to be defeated by a few factious persons using parliamentary forms with the evident object of obstructing business. In such a case he should refuse to entertain the dilatory or frivolous motion, and, if an appeal is taken, he should entertain it, and, if sustained by a large majority he may afterwards refuse to entertain even an appeal made by the faction when evidently made merely to obstruct business. But the chair should never adopt such a course merely to expedite business, when the opposition is not factious. It is only justifiable when it is perfectly clear that the opposition is trying to obstruct business. [See Dilatory Motions, **40**].

If it is necessary for the chairman to vacate the chair the first Vice President, if there is one, should take the chair, and in his absence the next one in order should take it. If there is no vice president in the hall, then the chairman may, if it is necessary to vacate the chair, appoint a chairman *pro tem.*, but the first adjournment puts an end to the appointment, which the assembly can terminate before, if it pleases, by electing another chairman. But the regular chairman, knowing that he will be absent from a future meeting, cannot authorize another member to act in his place at such meeting; the secretary, or, in his absence, some other member should in such case call the meeting to order, and a chairman *pro tem.* be elected who would hold office during that session, unless such office is terminated by the entrance of the president or a vice president, or by the election of another chairman *pro tem.*, which may be done by a majority vote.

The chairman sometimes calls a member to the chair and takes part in the debate. This should rarely be done, and nothing can justify it in a case where much feeling is shown and there is a liability to difficulty in preserving order. If the chairman has even the appearance of being a partisan, he loses much of his ability to control those who are on the opposite side of the question. There is nothing to justify the unfortunate habit some chairmen have of constantly speaking on questions before the assembly, even interrupting the member who has the floor. One who expects to take an active part in debate should never accept the chair, or at least should not resume the chair, after having made his speech, until after the pending question is disposed of.* The presiding officer of a large assembly should never be chosen for any reason except his ability to preside.

The chairman should not only be familiar with parliamentary usage, and set the example of strict conformity thereto, but he should be a man of executive ability, capable of controlling men. He should set an example of courtesy, and should never forget that to control others it is necessary to control one's self. A nervous, excited chairman can scarcely fail to cause trouble in a meeting. No rules will take the place of tact and common sense on the part of the chairman. While usually he need not wait for motions of routine, or for a motion to be seconded when he knows it is favored by others, yet if this is objected to, it is safer instantly to require the forms of parliamentary law to be observed By general consent many things can be done that will save much time [see page 202], but where the assembly is very large, or is divided and contains members who are habitually raising points of order, the most expeditious and safe course is to enforce strictly all the rules and forms of parliamentary law. He should be specially careful after every motion is made and every vote is taken to announce the next business in order. Whenever an improper motion is made, instead of simply ruling it out of order, it is well for the chairman to suggest how the desired object can be accomplished. [See "Hints to Inexperienced Chairman" below.]

The by-laws sometimes state that the president shall appoint all committees. In such case the assembly

---

* "Though the Speaker (Chairman) may of right speak to matters of order and be first heard, he is restrained from speaking on any other subject except where the House have occasion for facts within his knowledge; then he may, with their leave, state the matter of fact." [Jefferson's Manual, sec. XVII.]

"It is a general rule in all deliberative assemblies, that the presiding officer shall not participate in the debate, or other proceedings, in any other capacity than as such officer. He is only allowed, therefore, to state matters of fact within his knowledge; to inform the assembly on points of order or the course of proceeding, when called upon for that purpose, or when he finds it necessary to do so; and, on appeals from his decision on questions of order, to address the assembly in debate. [Cushing's Manual, §202.]

may authorize committees, but cannot appoint or nominate them. The president, however, cannot appoint any committees except those authorized by the by-laws or by a vote of the assembly. Sometimes the by-laws make the president ex-officio a member of every committee. Where this is done he has the rights of other members of the committees but not the obligation to attend every committee meeting. [See **51.**]

A chairman will often find himself perplexed with the difficulties attending his position, and in such cases he will do well to remember that parliamentary law was made for deliberative assemblies, and not the assemblies for parliamentary law. This is well expressed by a distinguished English writer on parliamentary law, thus: *"The great purpose of all rules and forms is to subserve the will of the assembly rather than to restrain it; to facilitate, and not to obstruct, the expression of their deliberative sense."*

Additional Duties of the President of a Society, and the Vice Presidents. In addition to his duties as presiding officer, in many societies the president has duties as an administrative or executive officer. Where this is desired, the by-laws should clearly set forth these duties, as they are outside of his duties as presiding officer of the assembly, and do not come within the scope of parliamentary law.

The same is true of vice presidents. Sometimes they have charge of different departments of work, and they should be chosen with those duties in view as prescribed by the by-laws. It must not be forgotten that in the case of the absence of the president the first vice president must preside, and in case of the illness or resignation or death of the president that the first vice president becomes president for the unexpired term, unless the rules specify how vacancies shall be filled. In such case the second vice president becomes the first, and so on. It is a mistake to elect a vice president who is not competent to perform the duties of president.

Hints to Inexperienced Chairmen. While in the chair, have beside you your Constitution, By-laws, and Rules of Order, which should be studied until you are perfectly familiar with them. You cannot tell the moment you may need this knowledge. If a member asks what motion to make in order to attain a certain object, you should be able to tell him at once. [**10.**] You should memorize the list of ordinary motions arranged in their order of precedence [page 7], and should be able to refer to the Table of Rules [page 8] so quickly that there will be no delay in deciding all points contained in it. Become familiar with the first ten sections of these Rules; they are simple, and will enable you more quickly to master parliamentary law. Read carefully sections **69-71**, so as to become accustomed to the ordinary methods of conducting business in deliberative assemblies. Notice that there are different ways of doing the same thing, all of which are allowable.

You should know all the business to come regularly before the meeting, and call for it in its regular order. Have with you a list of members of all committees, to guide you in nominating new committees.

When a motion is made, do not recognize any member or allow any one to speak until the motion is seconded and you have stated the question; or, in case of there being no second and no response to your call for a second, until you have announced that fact; except in case of a main motion before it is seconded or stated some one rises and says he rises to move a reconsideration, or to call up the motion to reconsider, or to move to take a question from the table. In any of these cases you should recognize the interrupting member as entitled to the floor [**3**]. If you have made a mistake and assigned the floor to the wrong person, or recognized a motion that was not in order, correct the error as soon as your attention is called to it. So, when a vote is taken, announce the result and also what question, if any, is then pending, before recognizing any member that addresses the chair. Never wait for mere routine motions to be seconded, when you know no one objects to them. [See **8.**]

If a member ignorantly makes an improper motion, do not rule it out of order, but courteously suggest the proper one. If it is moved "to lay the question on the table until 3 P. M.," as the motion is improper, ask if the intention is "to postpone the question to 3 P. M.;" if the answer is yes, then state that the question is on the postponement to that time. If it is moved simply "to postpone the question," without stating the time, do not rule it out of order, but ask the mover if he wishes "to postpone the question indefinitely" (which kills it), or "to lay it on the table" (which enables it to be taken up at any other time); then state the question in accordance with the motion he intended to make. So, if after a report has been presented and read, a member moves that "it be received," ask him if he means to move "its adoption" (or "acceptance," which is the same thing), as the report has been already received. No vote should be taken on receiving a report, which merely brings it before the assembly, and allows it to be read, unless some one objects to its reception.

The chairman of a committee usually has the most to say in reference to questions before the committee; but the chairman of an ordinary deliberative assembly, especially a large one, should, of all the members, have the least to say upon the merits of pending questions.

Never interrupt members while speaking, simply because you know more about the matter than they do; never get excited; never be unjust to the most troublesome member, or take advantage of his ignorance of parliamentary law, even though a temporary good is accomplished thereby.

Know all about parliamentary law, but do not try to show off your knowledge. Never be technical, or more strict than is absolutely necessary for the good of the meeting. Use your judgment; the assembly may be of such a nature through its ignorance of parliamentary usages and peaceable disposition, that a strict enforcement of the rules, instead of assisting, would greatly hinder business; but in large assemblies, where there is much work to be done, and especially where there is liability to trouble, the only safe course is to require a strict observance of the rules.

59. Secretary, or Clerk. The recording officer is variously called Clerk, or Secretary, or Recording Secretary (where there is also a Corresponding Secretary), or Recorder, or Scribe, etc. The secretary is the recording officer of the assembly and the custodian of its records except such as are specifically assigned to others, as the treasurer's books. These records are open, however, to inspection by any member at reasonable times, and where a committee needs any records of a society for the proper performance of its duties, they should be turned over to its chairman. The same principle applies in boards and committees, their records being accessible to members of the board or committee, as the case may be, but to no others.

In addition to keeping the records of the society and the minutes of the meetings, it is the duty of the secretary to keep a register, or roll, of the members and to call the roll when required; to notify officers, committees, and delegates of their appointment, and to furnish committees with all papers referred to them, and delegates with credentials; and to sign with the president all orders on the treasurer authorized by the society, unless otherwise specified in the by-laws. He should also keep one book in which the constitution, by-laws, rules of order, and standing rules should all be written, leaving every other page blank; and whenever an amendment is made to any of them, in addition to being recorded in the minutes it should be immediately entered on the page opposite to the article amended, with a reference, in red ink, to the date and page of the minutes where it is recorded.

In addition to the above duties, when there is only one secretary, it is his duty to send out proper notices of all called meetings, and of other meetings when necessary, and to conduct the correspondence of the society, except as otherwise provided. Where there is a *Corresponding Secretary* these duties devolve on him, as well as such others as are prescribed by the by-laws. The by-laws should always clearly define the additional duties of the corresponding secretary if any are to be imposed on him. When the word "secretary" is used it always refers to the recording secretary if there is more than one.

The secretary should, previous to each meeting, for the use of the chairman, make out an order of business [65], showing in their exact order what is necessarily to come before the assembly. He should also have, at each meeting, a list of all standing committees, and such special committees as are in existence at the time, as well as the by-laws of the organization and its minutes. His desk should be near that of the chairman, and in the absence of the chairman (if there is no vice president present), when the hour for opening the session arrives, it is his duty to call the meeting to order, and to preside until the election of a chairman *pro tem.*, which should take place immediately. He should keep a record of the proceedings, stating what was done and not what was said, unless it is to be published, and never making criticisms, favorable or otherwise, on anything said or done. This record, usually called the minutes, is kept as explained in the next section. When a committee is appointed, the secretary should hand the names of the committee, and all papers referred to it, to the chairman of the committee, or some other of its members. He should indorse on the reports of committees the date of their reception, and what further action was taken upon them, and preserve them among the records, for which he is responsible. It is not necessary to vote that a report be "placed on file," as that should be done without a vote, except in organizations that habitually keep no records except their minutes and papers ordered on file.

60. The Minutes. The record of the proceedings of a deliberative assembly is usually called the Minutes, or the Record, or the Journal. The essentials of the record are as follows: (*a*) the kind of meeting, "regular" (or stated) or "special," or "adjourned regular" or "adjourned special"; (*b*) name of the assembly; (*c*) date of meeting and place, when it is not always the same; (*d*) the fact of the presence of the regular chairman and secretary, or in their absence the names of their substitutes; (*e*) whether the minutes of the previous meeting were approved, or their reading dispensed with, the dates of the meetings being given when it is customary to occasionally transact business at other than the regular business meetings; (*f*) all the main motions (except such as were withdrawn) and points of order and appeals, whether sustained or lost, and all other motions that were not lost or withdrawn; (*g*) and usually the hours of meeting and adjournment, when the meeting is solely for business. Generally the name is recorded of the member who introduced a main motion, but not of the seconder.

In some societies the minutes are signed by the president in addition to the secretary, and when published they should always be signed by both officers. If minutes are not habitually approved at the next meeting, then there should be written at the end of the minutes the word "Approved" and the date of the approval, which should be signed by the secretary. They should be entered in good black ink in a well-bound record-book.*

The *Form* of the *Minutes* may be as follows:

At a regular meeting of the M. L. Society, held in their hall, on Thursday evening, March 19, 1914, the president in the chair, and Mr. N acting as secretary, the minutes of the previous meeting were read and approved. The Committee on Applications reported the names of Messrs. C and D as applicants for membership, and on motion of Mr. F they were admitted as members. The committee on .... reported through Mr. G a series of resolutions, which were thoroughly discussed and amended, and finally adopted, as follows:

Resolved, That ....

....

On motion of Mr. L the society adjourned at 10 P. M.

R......... N.............

Secretary.

In keeping the minutes, much depends upon the kind of meeting, and whether the minutes are to be published. In the meetings of ordinary societies and of boards of managers and trustees, there is no object in reporting the debates; the duty of the secretary, in such cases, is mainly to record what is "done" by the

* In many organizations it is preferable for the secretary to keep his original pencil notes in a pocket memorandum book which he carries to every meeting, and these original notes, as corrected, are approved and then copied into the permanent records. This plan usually results in neater records, but the original notes should be kept until they are carefully compared with the permanent records. In such case it is better to have the minutes signed by both president and secretary as a guarantee against errors in copying.

assembly, and not what is said by the members. He should enter the essentials of a record, as previously stated, and when a count has been ordered or where the vote is by ballot, he should enter the number of votes on each side; and when the voting is by yeas and nays he should enter a list of the names of those voting on each side. The proceedings of the committee of the whole, or while acting as if in committee of the whole, should not be entered in the minutes, but the report of the committee should be entered. When a question is considered informally, the proceedings should be kept as usual, as the only informality is in the debate. If a report containing resolutions has been agreed to, the resolutions should be entered in full as finally adopted by the assembly, thus: "The committee on .... submitted a report with a series of resolutions which, after discussion and amendment, were adopted as follows:" then should be entered the resolutions as adopted. Where the proceedings are published, the method shown further on should be followed. If the report is of great importance the assembly should order it "to be entered on the minutes," in which case the secretary copies it in full upon the record.

Where the regular meetings are held weekly, monthly, or quarterly, the minutes are read at the opening of each day's meeting, and, after correction, should be approved. Where the meetings are held several days in succession with recesses during the day, the minutes are read at the opening of business each day. If the next meeting of the organization will not be held for a long period, as six months or a year, the minutes that have not been read previously should be read and approved before final adjournment. If this is impracticable, then the executive committee, or a special committee, should be authorized to correct and approve them. In this case the record should be signed as usual, and after the signatures the word "Approved," with the date and the signature of the chairman of the committee authorized to approve them. At the next meeting, six months later, they need not be read, unless it is desired for information, as it is too late to correct them intelligently. When the reading of the minutes is dispensed with they can afterwards be taken up at any time when nothing is pending. If not taken up previously, they come before the assembly at the next meeting before the reading of the later minutes. With this exception the motion to dispense with reading the minutes is practically identical with the motion to lay the minutes on the table, being undebatable and requiring only a majority vote. The minutes of a secret meeting, as for the trial of a member, should not be read at a meeting that is open to the public, if the record contains any of the details of the trial that should not be made public.

Minutes to be Published. When the minutes are to be published, in addition to the strict record of what is done, as heretofore described, they should contain a list of the speakers on each side of every question, with an abstract of all addresses, if not the addresses in full, when written copies are furnished. In this case the secretary should have an assistant. With some annual conventions it is desired to publish the proceedings in full. In such cases it is necessary to employ a stenographer as assistant to the secretary. Reports of committees should be printed exactly as submitted, the minutes showing what action was taken by the assembly in regard to them; or, they may be printed with all additions in italics and parts struck out enclosed in brackets, in which case a note to that effect should precede the report or resolutions. In this way the reader can see exactly what the committee reported and also exactly what the assembly adopted or endorsed.

61. The Executive Secretary is usually a salaried officer paid to give up all his time to the work as executive officer, or general manager, of an organization under a board of managers and an executive committee [**50**]. In some organizations this officer is called Corresponding Secretary, but the title of corresponding secretary does not carry with it any duty except that of conducting the correspondence of the society as explained on page 246, unless it is prescribed by the by-laws. The office of the executive secretary is usually the only office of the organization, and there the Executive Committee meets and transacts its business. The board of managers in such cases is usually large and so scattered as never to have regular meetings oftener than quarterly. When the organization is a national one it usually meets just before the annual convention, when it hears the annual report, prepared by the executive secretary and previously adopted by the executive committee, and acts upon it. The new board meets immediately after the convention, and organizes, elects an executive committee and an executive secretary, when so authorized by the by-laws, and decides upon the general policy for the year, leaving the details to the executive committee and the executive secretary. The board rarely meets oftener than once or twice in addition to the meetings in connection with the annual meeting, special meetings, however, being called, when required, as provided by its by-laws. In some organizations the executive secretary is elected by the convention. He is usually ex-officio secretary of the executive committee. The members of the executive committee giving their time gratuitously, it is the duty of the executive secretary to prepare for the committee all business that has not been assigned to others, and to see that all its instructions are carried out. He is expected to recommend plans of work and conduct the business generally, under the executive committee, and prepare the annual report, which, after being adopted by the executive committee, should be adopted by the board, whose report it is, and then be submitted to the convention.

62. **Treasurer.** The duties of this officer vary in different societies. In probably the majority of cases he acts as a banker, merely holding the funds deposited with him and paying them out on the order of the society signed by the president and the secretary. He is always required to make an annual report, and in many societies he also makes a quarterly report which may be in the form given below. If the society has auditors the report should be handed to them, with the vouchers, in time

to be audited before the meeting. The auditors having certified to its correctness, submit their report, and the chair puts the question on adopting it, which has the effect of approving the treasurer's report, and relieving him from responsibility in case of loss of vouchers, except in case of fraud. If there are no auditors the report when made should be referred to an auditing committee, who should report on it later.

It should always be remembered that the financial report is made for the information of members. The details of dates and separate payments for the same object are a hindrance to its being understood, and are useless, as it is the duty of the auditing committee to examine into details and see if the report is correct. The best form for these financial reports depends upon the kind of society, and is best determined by examining those made in similar societies. The following brief report is in a form adapted to many societies where the financial work is a very subordinate part of their work:

REPORT OF THE TREASURER OF THE M. L. SOCIETY FOR THE QUARTER ENDING MARCH 31, 1914.

Receipts.

Balance on hand January 1, 1914....		$ 25.75
Initiation fees	$ 50.00	
Members' dues	150.00	
Fines	10.50	210.50
Total.........................		$236.25

Disbursements.

Rent of Hall........................	$ 80.00	
Electric lights	22.00	
Stationery and Printing.............	15.00	
Repair of Furniture................	10.00	
Janitor	60.00	$187.00
Balance on hand March 31, 1914..		49.25
Total..........................		$236.25

S........ M................,
Treasurer.

Examined and found correct.

R...... V............ }
J...... L............ } Auditing Committee.

Art. XI. Miscellaneous.

63. **A Session** of an assembly is a meeting which, though it may last for days, is virtually *one meeting*, as a session of a convention; or even months, as a session of Congress; it terminates by an "adjournment sine díe (without day)." The intermediate adjournments from day to day, or the recesses taken during the day, do not destroy the continuity of the meetings, which in reality constitute one session.

Any meeting which is not an adjournment of another meeting commences a new session. In the case of a permanent society, whose by-laws provide for regular meetings every week, month, or year, for example, each meeting constitutes a separate session of the society, which session, however, can be prolonged by adjourning to another day.

In this Manual the term *Meeting* is used to denote an assembling of the members of a deliberative assembly for any length of time, during which there is no separation of the members except for a recess of a few minutes, as the morning meetings, the afternoon meetings, and the evening meetings, of a convention whose session lasts for days. A "meeting" of an assembly is terminated by a temporary adjournment or a recess for a meal, etc.; a "session" of an assembly ends with an adjournment without day, and may consist of many meetings. So an adjournment to meet again at some other time, even the same day, unless it was for only a few minutes, terminates the meeting, but not the session, which latter includes all the adjourned meetings. The next meeting, in this case, would be an "adjourned meeting" of the same session.

In ordinary practice a meeting is closed by moving simply "to adjourn;" the society meets again at the time provided either by the rules or by a resolution of the society. If it does not meet till the time for the next regular meeting as provided in the by-laws, then the adjournment closes the session, and was in effect an adjournment without day. If, however, it had previously fixed the time for the next meeting, either by a direct vote or by adopting a program of exercise covering several meetings, or even days, in either case the adjournment is in effect to a certain time, and while closing the meeting does not close the session.

In such common expressions as quarterly meeting and annual meeting the word meeting is used in the sense of the parliamentary *session,* and covers all the adjourned meetings. Thus, business that legally must be done at the annual meeting may be done at any time during the session beginning at the time specified for the annual meeting, though the session, by repeated adjournments, may last for days. The business may be postponed to the next regular meeting, if desired.

Under Renewal of Motions [38] is explained what motions can be repeated during the same session, and also the circumstances under which certain motions cannot be renewed until after the close of the next succeeding session.

A rule or resolution of a permanent nature may be adopted by a majority vote at any session of a society, and it will continue in force until it is rescinded. But such a standing rule does not materially interfere with the rights of a future session, as by a majority vote it may be suspended so far as it affects that session; and, it may be rescinded by a majority vote, if notice of the proposed action was given at a previous meeting, or in the notice of the meeting; or, without any notice, it may be rescinded by a majority of the entire membership, or by a two-thirds vote. If it is desired to give greater stability to a rule it is necessary to place it in the constitution, by-laws, or rules of order, all of which are so guarded by requiring notice of amendments, and at least a two-thirds vote for their adoption, that they are not subject to sudden changes, and may be considered as expressing the deliberate views of the whole society, rather than the opinions or wishes of any particular meeting.

In case of the illness of the presiding officer the assembly cannot elect a chairman *pro tem.* to hold office beyond the session, unless notice of the election was given at the previous meeting or in the call for this meeting. So it is improper for an assembly to postpone anything to a day beyond the next succeeding session, and thus attempt to prevent the next session from considering the question. On the other hand, it is not permitted to move the reconsideration of a vote taken at a previous session, though the motion to reconsider can be called up, provided it was made during the previous session in a society having meetings as often as quarterly. Committees can be appointed to report at a future session.

NOTE ON SESSION.—In Congress, and in fact all legislative bodies, the limits of the sessions are clearly defined; but in ordinary societies having a permanent existence, with regular meetings more or less frequent, there appears to be some confusion upon the subject. Any society is competent to decide what shall constitute one of its sessions, but, where there is no rule on the subject, the common parliamentary law would make each of its regular or special meetings a separate session, as they are regarded in this Manual.

The disadvantages of a rule making a session include all the meetings of an ordinary society, held during a long time, as one year, are very great. If an objection to the consideration of a question has been sustained, or if a question has been adopted, or rejected, or postponed indefinitely, the question cannot again be brought before the assembly for its consideration during the same session. If a session lasted for a long period, a temporary majority could forestall the permanent majority, and introduce and act on a number of questions favored by the majority, and thus prevent the society from dealing with those subjects for the long period of the session. If members of any society take advantage of the freedom allowed by considering each regular meeting a separate session, and repeatedly renew obnoxious or unprofitable motions, the society can adopt a rule prohibiting the second introduction of any main question within, say, three months after its rejection, or indefinite postponement, or after the society has refused to consider it. But generally it is better to suppress the motion by refusing to consider it [**23**].

64. A Quorum of an assembly is such a number as must be present in order that business can be legally transacted. The quorum refers to the number present, not to the number voting. The quorum of a mass meeting is the number present at the time, as they constitute the membership at that time. The quorum of a body of delegates, unless the by-laws provide for a smaller quorum, is a majority of the number enrolled as attending the convention, not those appointed. The quorum of any other deliberative assembly with an enrolled membership (unless the by-laws provide for a smaller quorum) is a majority of all the members. In the case, however, of a society, like many religious ones, where there are no annual dues, and where membership is for life (unless it is transferred or the names are struck from the roll by a vote of the society) the register of members is not reliable as a list of the bona fide members of the society, and in many such societies it would be impossible to have present at a business meeting a majority of those enrolled as members. Where such societies have no by-law establishing a quorum, the quorum consists of those who attend the meeting, provided it is either a stated meeting or one that has been properly called.

In all ordinary societies the by-laws should provide for a quorum as large as can be depended upon for being present at all meetings when the weather is not exceptionally bad. In such an assembly the chairman should not take the chair until a quorum is present, or there is no prospect of there being a quorum. The only business that can be transacted in the absence of a quorum is to take measures to obtain a quorum, to fix the time to which to adjourn, and to adjourn, or to take a recess. Unanimous consent cannot be given when a quorum is not present, and a notice given then is not valid. In the case of an annual meeting, where certain business for the year, as the election of officers, must be attended to during the session, the meeting should fix a time for an adjourned meeting and then adjourn.

In an assembly that has the power to compel the attendance of its members, if a quorum is not present at the appointed hour, the chairman should wait a few minutes before taking the chair. In the absence of a quorum such an assembly may order a call of the house [41] and thus compel attendance of absentees, or it may adjourn, providing for an adjourned meeting if it pleases.

In committee of the whole the quorum is the same as in the assembly; if it finds itself without a quorum it can do nothing but rise and report to the assembly, which then adjourns. In any other committee the majority is a quorum, unless the assembly order otherwise, and it must wait for a quorum before proceeding to business. Boards of trustees, managers, directors, etc., are on the same footing as committees as regards a quorum. Their power is delegated to them as a body, and their quorum, or what number shall be present, in order that they may act as a board or committee, cannot be determined by them, unless so provided in the by-laws.

While no question can be decided in the absence of a quorum excepting those mentioned above, a member cannot be interrupted while speaking in order to make the point of no quorum. The debate may continue in the absence of a quorum until some one raises the point while no one is speaking.

While a quorum is competent to transact any business, it is usually not expedient to transact important business unless there is a fair attendance at the meeting, or else previous notice of such action has been given.

Care should be taken in amending the rule providing for a quorum. If the rule is struck out first, then the quorum instantly becomes a majority of all the members, so that in many societies it would be nearly impracticable to secure a quorum to adopt a new rule. The proper way is to amend by striking out certain words (or the whole rule) and inserting certain other words (or the new rule), which is made and voted on as one question.

Note on Quorum.—After all the members of an organization have had reasonable notice of a meeting, and ample opportunity for discussion, if a majority of the total membership of the organization come to a certain decision, that must be accepted as the action or opinion of that body. But, with the exception of a body of delegates, it is seldom that a vote as great as a majority of the total membership of a large voluntary organization can be obtained for anything, and consequently there has been established a common parliamentary law principle, that if a bare majority of the membership is present at a meeting properly called or provided for, a majority vote (which means a majority of those who vote) shall be sufficient to make the act the act of the body, unless it suspends a rule or a right of a member (as the right to introduce questions and the right of free discussion before being required to vote on finally disposing of a question) and that a two-thirds vote shall have the power to suspend these rules and rights. This gives the right to act for the society to about one-fourth of its members in ordinary cases, and to about one-third of its members in case of suspending the rules and certain rights. But it has been found impracticable to accomplish the work of most voluntary societies if no business can be transacted unless a majority of the members is present. In large organizations, meeting weekly or monthly for one or two hours, it is the exception when a majority of the members is present at a meeting, and therefore it has been found necessary to require the presence of only a small percentage of the members to enable the assembly to act for the organization, or, in other words, to establish a small quorum. In legislative bodies in this country, which are composed of members paid for their services, it is determined by the constitutions to be a majority of their members. Congress in 1861 decided this to be a majority of the members chosen. In the English House of Commons it is 40 out of nearly 700, being about 6% of the members, while in the House of Lords the quorum is 3, or about one-half of 1% of the members. Where the quorum is so small it has been found necessary to require notice of all bills, amendments, etc., to be given in advance; and even in Congress, with its large quorum, one day's notice has to be given of any motion to rescind or change any rule or standing order. This principle is a sound one, particularly with societies meeting monthly or weekly for one or two hours, and with small quorums, where frequently the assembly is no adequate representation of the society. The difficulty in such cases may be met in societies adopting this Manual by the proper use of the motion to reconsider and have entered on the minutes as explained on page 165.

65. Order of Business. It is customary for every society having a permanent existence to adopt an order of business for its meetings. When no rule has been adopted, the following is the order:

(1) Reading the Minutes of the previous meeting [and their approval].
(2) Reports of Boards and Standing Committees.
(3) Reports of Special (Select) Committees.
(4) Special Orders.
(5) Unfinished Business and General Orders.
(6) New Business.

The minutes are read only once a day at the beginning of the day's business. The second item includes the reports of all Boards of Managers, Trustees, etc., as well as reports of such officers as are required to make them. The fifth item includes, first, the business pending and undisposed of at the previous adjournment; and then the general orders that were on the calendar for the previous meeting and were not disposed of; and finally, matters postponed to this meeting that have not been disposed of.

The secretary should always have at every meeting a memorandum of the order of business for the use of the presiding officer, showing everything that is to come before the meeting. The chairman, as soon as one thing is disposed of, should announce the next business in order. When reports are in order he should call for the different reports in their order, and when unfinished business is in order he should announce the different questions in their proper order, as stated above, and thus always keep the control of the business.

If it is desired to transact business out of its order, it is necessary to suspend the rules

[22], which can be done by a two-thirds vote But, as each resolution or report comes up, a majority can at once lay it on the table, and thus reach any question which it desires first to dispose of. It is improper to lay on the table or to postpone a class of questions like reports of committees, or in fact anything but the question before the assembly.

66. Nominations and Elections. Before proceeding to an election to fill an office it is customary to nominate one or more candidates. This nomination is not necessary when the election is by ballot or roll call, as each member may vote for any eligible person whether nominated or not. When the vote is viva voce or by rising, the nomination is like a motion to fill a blank, the different names being repeated by the chair as they are made, and then the vote is taken on each in the order in which they were nominated, until one is elected. The nomination need not be seconded. Sometimes a nominating ballot is taken in order to ascertain the preferences of the members. But in the election of the officers of a society it is more usual to have the nominations made by a committee. When the committee makes its report, which consists of a ticket, the chair asks if there are any other nominations, when they may be made from the floor. The committee's nominations are treated just as if made by members from the floor, no vote being taken on accepting them. When the nominations are completed the assembly proceeds to the election, the voting being by any of the methods mentioned under Voting, [46], unless the by-laws prescribe a method. The usual method in permanent societies is by ballot, the balloting being continued until the offices are all filled. An election takes effect immediately if the candidate is present and does not decline, or if he is absent and has consented to his candidacy. If he is absent and has not consented to his candidacy, it takes effect when he is notified of his election, provided he does not decline immediately. After the election has taken effect and the officer or member has learned the fact, it is too late to reconsider the vote on the election. An officer-elect takes possession of his office immediately, unless the rules specify the time. In most societies it is necessary that this time be clearly designated.

67. Constitutions, By-laws, Rules of Order, and Standing Rules. The rules of a society, in a majority of cases, may be conveniently divided into these four classes, though in some societies all the rules are found under one of these heads, being called either the constitution, or the by-laws, or the standing rules.

Such provisions in regard to the constitution, etc., as are of a temporary nature should not be placed in the constitution, etc., but should be included in the motion to adopt, thus: "I move the adoption of the constitution reported by the committee and that the four directors receiving the most votes shall serve for three years, the four receiving the next largest numbers shall serve for two years, and the next four for one year, and that where there is a tie the classification shall be by lot;" or, "I move the adoption, etc....... and that Article III, shall not go into effect until after the close of this annual meeting." Or, if the motion to adopt has been made, it may be amended so as to accomplish the desired object.

Constitutions. An incorporated society frequently has no constitution, the charter taking its place, and many others prefer to combine under one head the rules that are more commonly placed under the separate heads of constitution and by-laws. There is no objection to this unless the by-laws are elaborate, when it is better to separate the most important rules and place them in the constitution. The constitution should contain only the following:

(1) Name and object of the society.
(2) Qualification of members.
(3) Officers and their election.
(4) Meetings of the society (including only what is essential, leaving details to the by-laws).
(5) How to amend the constitution.

These can be arranged in five articles, or, the first one may be divided into two, in which case there would be six articles. Usually some of the articles should be divided into sections. Nothing should be placed in the constitution that may be suspended, except in the case of requiring elections of officers to be by ballot, in which case the requirement may be qualified so as to allow the ballot to be dispensed with by a unanimous vote when there is but one candidate for the office. The officers and board of managers or directors of an organization that meets only annually in convention, and the chairmen of such committees as it has authorized and has required to report to the convention, should be, if present at the convention, ex-officio members thereof, and provision for this should be made in the constitution. The constitution should require previous notice of an amendment and also a two-thirds or three-fourths vote for its adoption. Where the meetings are frequent, an amendment should not be allowed to be made except at a quarterly or annual meeting, after having been proposed at the previous quarterly meeting. [See Amendments to Constitutions, etc., 68.]

By-laws should include all the rules that are of such importance that they cannot be changed in any way without previous notice, except those placed in the constitution and the rules of order. Few societies adopt any special rules of order of their own under that name, contenting themselves with putting a few such rules in their by-laws and then adopting some standard work on parliamentary law as their authority. When a society is incorporated the charter may take the place of the constitution, and in such a case the by-laws would contain all the rules of the society, except those in the charter that cannot be changed without previous notice. The by-laws should always provide for their amendment as shown in **68**, and also for a quorum, **64**. If it is desired to permit the suspension of any by-law it should be specifically provided for. By-laws, except those relating to business procedure, cannot be suspended, unless they expressly provide for their suspension. By-laws in the nature of rules of order may be suspended by a two-thirds vote, as stated in **22**.

The duties of the presiding and recording officers of a deliberative assembly are defined in **58** and **59**. But in many societies other duties are required of the president and the secretary, and these, together with the duties of the other officers, if any, should be defined in the by-laws. If a society wishes to provide for honorary officers or members, it is well to do so in the by-laws. Unless the by-laws state the contrary, these positions are simply complimentary, carrying with them the right to attend the meetings and to speak, but not to make motions or to vote. Honorary presidents and vice presidents should sit on the platform, but they do not, by virtue of their honorary office, preside. An honorary office is not strictly an office, and in no way conflicts with a member's holding a real office, or being assigned any duty whatever, the same as if he did not hold the honorary office. Like a college honorary degree, it is perpetual, unless rescinded. So it is proper, where desired, to include in the published list of honorary officers the names of all upon whom the honor has been conferred, even though deceased.

Rules of Order should contain only the rules relating to the orderly transaction of business in the meetings and to the duties of the officers. There is no reason why most of these rules should not be the same for all ordinary societies, and there is a great advantage in uniformity of procedure, so far as possible, in all societies all over the country. Societies should, therefore, adopt some generally accepted rules of order, or parliamentary manual, as their authority, and then adopt only such special rules of order as are needed to supplement their parliamentary authority. Every society, in its by-laws or rules of order, should adopt a rule like this: "The rules contained in [specifying the work on parliamentary practice] shall govern the society in all cases to which they are applicable, and in which they are not inconsistent with the by-laws or the special rules of order of this society." Without such a rule, any one so disposed can cause great trouble in a meeting.

Standing Rules should contain only such rules as may be adopted without previous notice by a majority vote at any business meeting. The vote on their adoption, or their amendment, before or after adoption, may be reconsidered. At any meeting they may be suspended by a majority vote, or they may be amended or rescinded by a two-thirds vote. If notice of the proposed action was given at a previous meeting or in the call for this meeting, they may be amended or rescinded by a majority vote. As a majority may suspend any of them for that meeting, these rules do not interfere with the freedom of any meeting and therefore require no notice in order to adopt them. Generally they are not adopted at the organization of a society, but from time to time as they are needed. Sometimes the by-laws of a society are called standing rules, but it is better to follow the usual classification of rules as given in this section. The following is an example of a standing rule:

Resolved, That the meetings of this society from April 1 to September 30 shall begin at 7:30 P. M., and during the rest of the year at 8 P. M.

No standing rule, or resolution, or motion is in order that conflicts with the constitution, or by-laws, or rules of order, or standing rules.

68. Amendments of Constitutions, By-laws, and Rules of Order. Constitutions, by-laws, and rules of order, that have been adopted and contain no rule for their amendment, may be amended at any regular business meeting by a vote of the majority of the entire membership; or, if the amendment was submitted in writing at the previous regular business meeting, then they may be amended by a two-thirds vote of those voting, a quorum being present. But each society should adopt rules for the amendment of its constitution, by-laws, and rules of order, adapted to its own case, but always requiring previous notice and a two-thirds vote. Where assemblies meet regularly only once a year, the constitution, etc., should provide for copies of the amendment to be sent with the notices to the members or the constituency, instead of requiring amendments to be submitted at the previous annual meeting. The requirements should vary to suit the needs of each assembly, always providing for ample notice to the members or the constituency. In societies having very frequent meetings, and also monthly or quarterly meetings more especially devoted to business, it is well to allow amendments to the by-laws, etc., to be adopted only at the quarterly or annual meetings. In specifying when the amendment must be submitted, "*the* previous regular meeting" should be used instead of "*a* previous regular meeting," as in the latter case action on the amendment might be delayed indefinitely to suit the mover, and the object of giving notice be defeated. In prescribing the vote necessary for the adoption of an amendment, the expression "a vote of two-thirds of the members" should never be used in ordinary societies, especially in large organizations with quorums smaller than a majority of the membership, as in such societies it is seldom that two-thirds of the members—that is, two-thirds of the entire membership—is ever present at a meeting. If it is desired to require a larger vote than two-thirds (that is, two-thirds of the votes cast, a quorum being present), the expression "a vote of two-thirds of the members present," should be used. Instead of submitting the amendment in writing, sometimes only notice, or written notice, of an amendment is required. Unless the notice is required to be in writing it may be given orally. In any case, only the purport of the amendment is necessary, unless the rule requires that the amendment itself shall be submitted.

If a committee is appointed to revise the by-laws and report at a certain meeting, this would be all the notice required, and the amendments could be immediately acted upon, if the by-laws required only previous notice of an amendment. But if they required the amendment, or "notice of such amendment," to be submitted at the previous regular meeting, the revision could not be taken up until the next regular meeting after the committee had submitted its report. The committee may submit a substitute for the by-laws unless it is limited as to its report, as a substitute is an amendment. Great care should be exercised in amending constitutions, etc., to comply with every rule in regard to their amendment.

An amendment to the constitution, or anything else that has already been adopted, goes into effect immediately upon its adoption, unless the motion to adopt specifies a time for its going into effect, or the assembly has previously adopted a motion to that effect. While the amendment is pending, a motion may be made to amend by adding a proviso similar to this, "Provided, that this does not go into effect until after the close of this annual meeting." Or, while the amendment is pending, an incidental motion may be adopted that in case the amendment is adopted it shall not take effect until a specified time. This requires only a majority vote.

Amending a proposed amendment to the constitution, etc., may be accomplished by a majority vote, without notice, subject to certain restrictions. The assembly is not limited to adopting or rejecting the amendment just as it is proposed, but no amendment is in order that increases the modification of the rule to be amended, as otherwise advantage could be taken of this by submitting a very slight change that would not attract attention and then moving the serious modification as an amendment to the amendment.

Thus, if the by-laws placed the annual dues of members at $2.00, and an amendment is pending to strike out 2 and insert 5, an amendment would be in order to change the 5 to any number between 2 and 5; but an amendment would not be in order that changed the 5 to any number greater than 5 or less than 2. Had notice been given that it was proposed to increase the dues to more than 5 dollars, or to reduce them below 2 dollars, members might have been present to oppose the change, who did not attend because they were not opposed to an increase as high as 5 dollars. The same principle applies to an amendment in the nature of a substitute, the proposed substitute being open to amendments that diminish the changes, but not to amendments that increase those that are proposed, or introduce new changes. Thus, if an amendment is pending, substituting a new rule for one that prescribes the initiation fee and annual dues, and the substitute does not change the annual dues, then a motion to amend it so as to change the annual dues would be out of order. The notice must be sufficiently definite to give fair warning to all parties interested as to the exact points that are to be modified. The proposed amendment is a main motion, and that is the only question before the assembly. It is subject to amendments of the first and second degree, like other main motions, and no amendment that is not germane to it is in order.

A society can amend its constitution and by-laws so as to affect the emoluments and duties of officers already elected, or even to do away with the office altogether. If it is desired that the amendment should not affect officers already elected, a motion to that effect should be adopted before voting on the amendment; or the motion to amend could have added to it the proviso that it should not affect officers already elected. There is something in the nature of a contract between a society and its officers which either one can modify to some extent, or even terminate, but it must be done with reasonable consideration for the other party. A secretary, for instance, has no right to refuse to perform his duties on the ground that he has handed in his resignation. On the other hand, the society cannot compel him to continue in office beyond a reasonable time to allow for choosing his successor.

Care should be exercised in wording the sections providing for amending the constitution, etc., to avoid such tautology as "amend, or add to, or repeal," or "alter or amend," or "amend or in any way change." The one word "amend" covers any change whatever in the constitution, etc., whether it is a word or a paragraph that is added or struck out, or replaced by another word or paragraph, or whether a new constitution, etc., is substituted for the old one.

PART II.

Organization, Meetings, and Legal Rights of Assemblies.

Art. XII. Organization and Meetings.

69. **An Occasional or Mass Meeting.** (*a*) *Organization.* Before calling a meeting that is not one of an organized society, the following *Preliminary Steps* should be taken: Those who are responsible for the call should consult together and agree upon the place and time of the meeting, how the notice shall be given, who shall call the meeting to order and nominate the chairman, who shall be nominated for chairman, and who shall explain the object of the meeting. It is also good policy sometimes to have a set of resolutions drafted in advance to submit to the meeting.

It is not customary to call mass meetings to order promptly at the appointed time, but to wait ten or fifteen minutes, when the one chosen for the purpose steps to the front and says: "The meeting will please come to order; I move that Mr. A act as [or I nominate Mr. A for] chairman of this meeting." Some one else says, "I second the motion [or nomination]." The first member then puts the question to vote, by saying, "It has been moved and seconded that Mr. A act as [or Mr. A has been nominated for] chairman of this meeting; those in favor of the motion [or nomination] say *aye;*" and when the affirmative vote is taken, he says, "Those opposed say *no.*" If the majority vote is in the affirmative, he says, "The ayes have it, and Mr. A is elected chairman. He will please take the chair." If the motion is lost he announces that fact, and calls for the nomination of some one else for chairman, and proceeds with the new nomination as in the first case.

The member who calls the meeting to order, instead of making the motion himself, may act as temporary chairman, and say, "The meeting will please come to order; will some one nominate a chairman?" He puts the question to vote on the nomination as described above, or as below, in case of the secretary. This is dangerous, however, in large meetings, where an incompetent person may be nominated and elected chairman. In large assemblies, the member who nominates, with one other member, frequently conducts the presiding officer to the chair, and the chairman makes a short speech, thanking the assembly for the honor conferred on him.

When the chairman takes the chair he says, "The first business in order is the election of a secretary." Some one then makes a motion as just described, or he says, "I nominate Mr. B," when the chairman puts the question as below. Sometimes several names are called out, and the chairman, as he hears them, says, "Mr. B is nominated; Mr. C is nominated," etc.; he then takes the vote on the first one he heard, putting the question in a form similar to this: "As many as are in favor of Mr. B for secretary say *aye;* those opposed say *no.* The chair is in doubt: those in favor of Mr. B for secretary will rise; those opposed will rise. The negative has it and the motion is lost. As many as are in favor of Mr. C for secretary say *aye;* those opposed say *no.* The ayes have it, and Mr. C is elected secretary. He will please take his place at the desk." If Mr. C fails of election the vote is taken on the next nominee, and so on until one is elected. The secretary should take his seat near the chairman, and keep a record of the proceedings, as described in **59.** The chairman should always stand in putting the question to vote, and in large assemblies it is better for him to stand while stating the question. During debate he should be seated, and pay attention to the discussion. When nominations are made it is optional whether they are seconded or not. They are usually not debated, though sometimes the one making the nomination and the one seconding it say a few words at the time in favor of their nominee. A nomination cannot be amended. If additional officers are desired, they may be elected in the same manner as the secretary.

(*b*) *Adoption of Resolutions.* These two officers are all that are usually necessary, so as soon as the secretary is elected, the chairman directs the secretary to read the call for the meeting and then calls on the person most familiar with the question to explain the object of the meeting more fully, or he may do this himself. This explanation should be immediately followed by some one's offering a series of resolutions previously prepared, or by his moving the appointment of a committee to prepare resolutions upon the subject In the first case he rises and says, "Mr. Chairman;" the chairman responds, "Mr. C." Mr. C, having thus obtained the floor, says, "I move the adoption of the following resolutions," which he reads and hands to the chairman. Some one else says, "I second the motion." The chairman then says, "It has been moved and seconded to adopt the following resolutions," which he reads, or directs the secretary to read, and then says, "The question is on the adoption of the resolutions." If no one rises at once, he asks, "Are you ready for the question?" The resolutions are now open to debate and amendment. They may be referred to a committee, or may have any other subsidiary motion applied to them. When the debate appears to be finished, the chair again asks, "Are you ready for the question?" If no one then rises, he says, "As many as are in favor of the adoption of the resolutions say *aye;*" after the ayes have voted, he says, "As many as are of a contrary opinion [or are opposed] say *no;*" he then announces the result of the vote as follows: "The ayes have it [or the motion is carried] and the resolutions are adopted." If the debate has lasted any length of time, he should, before taking the vote, have the resolutions again read.

It is the practice, in legislative bodies, to send to the clerk's desk all resolutions, bills, etc., the title of the bill and the name of the member introducing it being indorsed on each. In such bodies, however, there are several clerks and only one chairman. In most assemblies there is but one clerk or secretary, and as he has to keep the minutes, there is no reason for his being constantly interrupted to read every resolution offered. In such assemblies, unless there is a rule or established custom to the contrary, it is usually much better to hand all resolutions, reports, etc., directly to the chairman. If they were read by the member introducing them, and no one calls for another reading, the chairman may omit reading them when he thinks they are fully understood. [For the manner of reading and stating the question when the resolution contains several paragraphs, see **24**.]

Dividing Resolutions. If the committee reports several independent resolutions relating to different subjects, the chair must state the question separately on the resolution, or resolutions, relating to each subject, on the request of a single member. If the resolutions relate to a single subject and yet each one is capable of standing alone if all the rest are rejected, they may be divided by a majority vote on a motion to divide the question, as explained in **24.** If the resolutions are so connected that they cannot stand alone, then the proper way to secure a separate vote on any objectionable resolution is to move to strike it out. When the chair states the question on striking it out, the resolution is open to amendments of the second degree, so as to perfect it, before the vote is taken on striking it out. [See page 140.]

Amending a Resolution. If it is desired to amend a pending resolution, that is, a resolution that the chair has stated as before the assembly for action, a member rises and obtains the floor as already described, and offers, or moves, his amendment, thus: "I move to insert the words 'with asphalt' after the word 'paved.'" If the motion is not at once seconded, the chair asks if the motion is seconded. In a large assembly he should repeat the motion before making this inquiry, as members who would be willing to second the motion may not have heard it. In fact, the chair must usually assume that some members do not hear what is said from the floor, and therefore that he must always repeat motions and the result of votes. The motion being seconded, the chair states the question thus: "It is moved and seconded to amend the resolution by inserting the words 'with asphalt' after the word 'paved.' Are you ready for the question?" The question is now open to debate and amendment, which must be confined, however, to the amendment, as it has superseded the resolution and has become what is termed the *immediately pending question.* If no one rises to claim the floor, the chair puts the question thus: "As many as are in favor of the amendment [or motion] say *aye;* those opposed say *no.* The ayes have it, and the amendment is adopted. The question is now on the resolution as amended, which is as follows [repeat the amended resolution]. Are you ready for the question?" The resolution is again open to debate and amendment, as it has again become the immediately pending question. When the chair thinks the debate ended, he asks, "Are you ready for the question?" If no one rises to claim the floor, he puts the question on the resolution, thus: "The question is on adopting the following resolution: *"Resolved,* That .... Those in favor of the motion [or, of adopting the resolution] say *aye;* those opposed say *no.* The ayes have it, and the resolution is adopted."

(*c*) *Committee to Draft Resolutions.* If it is preferred to appoint a committee to draft resolutions, a member, after he has addressed the chair and has been recognized, says: "I move that a committee of five be appointed by the chair to draft resolutions expressive of the sense of this meeting on," etc., adding the subject for which the meeting was called. The motion being seconded, the chairman states the question thus: "It has been moved and seconded that a committee of five be appointed by the chair to draft resolutions, etc. [repeat the motion]. Are you ready for the question?" If no one rises he may put the question thus: "As many as are in favor of the motion say *aye;* those opposed say *no.* The ayes have it and the motion is adopted." Or, it may be put thus: "The question is, 'Shall a committee of five be appointed by the chair to draft resolutions, etc. [repeating the motion]?' As many as are of the affirmative will raise their right hands. As many as are of the negative will signify it in the same way. The affirmative has it and the motion is adopted. The chair will appoint Messrs. A, B, C, D, and E as the committee on resolutions. The committee will withdraw and prepare the resolutions as quickly as possible. What is the further pleasure of the meeting?"

In a mass meeting, or in any very large assembly, it is safer to have all committees appointed by the chair. If the assembly, however, prefers a different method, the procedure is as described in **32**; or the following method may be adopted: A member moves, "That a committee be appointed to draft resolutions," etc. This motion being adopted, the chair asks: "Of how many shall the committee consist?" If only one number is suggested, he announces that the committee will consist of that number; if several numbers are suggested, he states the different ones, and then takes a vote on each, beginning with the largest, until one number is selected. He then inquires: "How shall the committee be appointed?" This is usually decided without the formality of a vote. The committee may be "appointed" by the chair, in which case the chairman names the committee, and no vote is taken; or the committee may be "nominated" by the chair, or by members of the assembly (no member naming more than one, except by unanimous consent), and then the assembly votes on their appointment. When the chairman nominates, after stating the names, he puts one question on the entire committee, thus: "As many as are in favor of these gentlemen constituting the committee say *aye,*" etc. If nominations are made by members of the assembly, and more names are mentioned than the number of the committee, a separate vote must be taken on each name, in the order of nomination, until the committee is filled.

When the committee is appointed, it should at once retire and agree upon a report, which should be written out as described in **52.** During its absence other business may be attended to, or the time may be occupied with hearing addresses. If the chairman sees the committee return to the room, he should announce, as soon as the pending business is disposed of, or the member speaking closes, that the assembly will now hear the report of the committee on resolutions: or, before this announcement he may ask if the committee is prepared to report. If the chairman does not notice the return of the committee, its chairman avails himself of the first opportunity to obtain the floor, when he says: "The committee appointed to draft resolutions is prepared to report." The chairman tells him that the assembly will now hear the report, which is then read by the chairman of the committee, who immediately moves its adoption, and then hands it to the presiding officer, upon which the committee is dissolved without any action of the assembly. The chairman then proceeds as stated above when the resolutions were offered by a member. If it is not desired immediately to adopt the resolutions, they may be debated, modified, their consideration postponed, etc., as explained in **10.**

When through with the business for which the assembly was convened, or when from any other cause it is desired to close the meeting, some one moves "to adjourn." If no time has been appointed for another meeting, this motion may be amended and debated as any other main motion. If the motion is carried, and no other time for meeting has been appointed, the chairman, in case the ayes and noes are nearly equal, says: "The ayes seem to have it, the ayes have it, the motion is adopted, and we stand adjourned without day (sine die)." If the vote is overwhelmingly in the affirmative, the expression, "The ayes seem to have it," should be omitted. If a time for an adjourned meeting has been appointed, the chair declares the assembly "adjourned to 8 o'clock next Wednesday evening," or whatever is the appointed time. Before declaring the adjournment, or even taking a vote on adjourning, the chair should satisfy himself that all required notices are given.

(*d*) *Semi-Permanent Mass Meetings.* Sometimes it is desirable to continue the mass meetings until a certain object is accomplished, and in such case the assembly may prefer to make a temporary organization at first, and then make their semi-permanent organization with more deliberation. If so, the assembly would be organized as just described, only adding "*pro tem.*" to the title of the officers, thus, "chairman *pro tem.*" The "*pro tem.*" is never used in addressing the officers. As soon as the secretary *pro tem.* is elected, a committee is usually appointed to nominate the semi-permanent officers, as in the case of a convention. A committee on rules should also be appointed, which should recommend a few rules providing for the time and place for holding the meetings, for some authority on parliamentary law, and for the number and length of speeches allowed, if two speeches not to exceed ten minutes each is not satisfactory.

Frequently the presiding officer is called the President, and sometimes there is a large number of Vice Presidents appointed for merely complimentary purposes. The Vice Presidents in large formal meetings sit on the platform beside the President, and in his absence, or when he vacates the chair, the first on the list that is present should take the chair.

70. A Permanent Society. (*a*) *First Meeting.* When it is desired to form a permanent society, those interested in it should consult together and carefully lay their plans before calling a meeting to organize the society. They should also be careful in calling the meeting to see to it that there is a majority in sympathy with their plans. By neglect of this, and giving a newspaper invitation to all interested in the object to attend the meeting, those who originated the work have found themselves in the minority and not in sympathy with the constitution which was adopted, so that they did not care to join the society after it was organized. Having taken all the preliminary steps, then, as described in case of a mass meeting [page 275], they invite those who they have reason to think are in sympathy with their general plans to meet at a certain time and place to consider the question of organizing a society for a certain purpose. As one of their preliminary steps they should procure copies of the constitutions and by-laws of several similar societies for the use of the committee in drafting their own.

It is not usual in meetings called to organize a society, or in mass meetings, to commence until ten or fifteen minutes after the appointed time, when the person previously selected for the purpose steps forward and says: "The meeting will please come to order; I move that Mr. A act as chairman of this meeting." Some one "seconds the motion," when the one who made the motion puts it to vote (or, as it is called, "puts the question"), as already described under a "mass meeting" [**69**]; and, as in that case, when the chairman is elected he takes the chair and announces, as the first business in order, the election of a secretary.

After the secretary is elected, the chairman calls on the member who is most interested in forming the society to state the object of the meeting. When this member rises he says, "Mr. Chairman." The chairman then announces his name, when the member proceeds to state the object of the meeting. Having finished his remarks, the chairman may call on other members to give their opinions on the subject, and sometimes a particular speaker is called out by members who wish to hear him. The chairman should observe the wishes of the assembly, and, while being careful not to be too strict, he must not permit any one to occupy too much time and weary the assembly.

When a sufficient time has been spent in this informal way, some one should offer a resolution, so that definite action can be taken. Those interested in arranging for the meeting, if it is to be a large one, should have previously agreed upon what is to be done, and be prepared, at the proper time, to offer a suitable resolution, which may be in form similar to this: "*Resolved,* That it is the sense of this meeting that a society for (state the object of the society) should now be formed in this city." This resolution, when seconded and stated by the chair, is open to debate and amendment, and is treated as already described [69]. This preliminary motion could have been offered at the commencement of the meeting, and if the meeting is a very large one this is generally better than to have the informal discussion.

After this preliminary motion has been voted on, or even without waiting for such a motion to be made, one like this may be offered: "I move that a committee of five be appointed by the chair to draft a constitution and by-laws for a society for (here state the object), and that it report at an adjourned meeting of this assembly." This motion can be amended by striking out and adding words, etc., and it is debatable.

When this committee is appointed, the chairman may inquire: "Is there any other business to be attended to?" or, "What is the further pleasure of the assembly [or club, or convention, etc.]?" When all business is finished, a motion may be made to adjourn to meet at a certain place and time, which, when seconded and stated by the chair, is open to debate and amendment. It is usually better to fix the time of the next meeting at an earlier stage of the meeting; and then, when it is desired to close the meeting, move simply "to adjourn," which cannot be amended or debated. When this motion is carried, the chairman says, "This meeting stands adjourned to meet at," etc., specifying the time and place of the next meeting.

(*b*) *Second Meeting.* At the next meeting the officers of the previous meeting, if present, serve until the permanent officers are elected. When the hour arrives for the meeting, the chairman, standing, says, "The meeting will please come to order;" as soon as the assembly is seated, he says, "The secretary will read the minutes of the last meeting," and then takes his seat. If any one notices an error in the minutes, he should state the fact as soon as the secretary finishes reading them; if there is no objection, without waiting for a motion, the chairman directs the secretary to make the correction. The chairman then says, "There being no [further] corrections, the minutes stand approved as read [or as corrected]."

The chair then announces, as the next business in order, the hearing of the report of the committee on the constitution and by-laws. The chairman of the committee, after addressing "Mr. Chairman" and being recognized, says something like this: "The committee appointed to draft a constitution and by-laws has agreed upon the following, and has directed me to report the same and move their adoption." He then reads them, moves their adoption, and hands them to the chair. The motion being seconded, the chair says: "It has been moved and seconded to adopt the constitution and by-laws reported by the committee. The question is on the adoption of the constitution, which will now be read." The constitution is then read from the platform by the secretary, or by the chairman of the committee, as the chair directs. This reading may be dispensed with by general consent, as it has already been read. He then reads, or has read, the first paragraph, and asks if there are any amendments proposed to this paragraph. When through with amending it he says, "There being no [further] amendments to this paragraph, the next will be read." No vote should be taken on adopting the separate paragraphs. He thus proceeds through the entire constitution, and then says the whole constitution is now open to amendment. This is the time to insert additional paragraphs, or make any amendments to the earlier paragraphs rendered necessary by changes made in the later ones.

When the chairman thinks the constitution has been modified to suit the wishes of the assembly, he inquires: "Are you ready for the question?" If no one wishes to speak, he puts the question: "As many as are in favor of adopting the constitution as amended say *aye;*" and then, "As many as are opposed say *no.*" He distinctly announces the result of the vote. This should never be omitted. Only a majority vote is required to adopt a constitution of a new society, or to amend it before it is adopted.

The chairman now states that the constitution having been adopted, it will be necessary for those wishing to become members to sign it (and pay the initiation fee, if required by the constitution), and, if the assembly is a large one, suggests that a recess be taken for the purpose. A motion is then made to take a recess for, say, ten minutes, or until the constitution is signed. The constitution being signed, no one is permitted to vote excepting those who have signed it, and thus have joined the society. While the payment of the initiation fee is strictly a prerequisite to the right to vote, it should be waived at this meeting with those who are unprepared to make the payment.

The recess having expired, the chairman calls the meeting to order, and says, "The secretary will read the roll of members." This is necessary in order that all may know who are entitled to take part in the future proceedings. After the roll has been read, the chair says, "The question before the assembly is on the adoption of the by-laws reported by the committee. The secretary will please read them." He then proceeds exactly as in the case of the constitution. The motion to adopt the constitution and by-laws reported by the committee having been made when the committee made its report, no further motion is necessary.

When the by-laws are adopted, the chair says, "The next business in order is the election of the permanent officers of the society." The by-laws should prescribe the method of nomination and election of the officers, and they should be strictly complied with. If the by-laws do not prescribe the method of nomination, the chair asks, "How shall the officers be nominated?" Some one may at once move that a committee be appointed by the chair to nominate the permanent officers of the society. This motion being adopted, the chair appoints the committee, which retires and agrees upon a ticket. During the absence of the committee the assembly may transact any business it pleases, or it may take a recess. When the committee returns to the hall, as soon as pending business is disposed of, the chair calls on the chairman of the committee for the report. The chairman of the committee reads the list of nominations, and hands it to the chair. The chair reads the list, and then asks, "Are there any further nominations?" Any member may now rise and, after addressing the chair, nominate any one else for any office, or he may nominate one person for each office, thus proposing a new ticket. The chair announces the nominations as made, and when he thinks that no more names will be proposed, he asks, "Are there any more nominations?" If there is no response, and if the by-laws prescribe that the election shall be by ballot, as they usually should, he appoints tellers and directs them to distribute blank ballots, upon which each member writes the name of each office and the person for whom he votes to fill that office. When the ballots are filled out, the chair directs the tellers to collect the ballots, which they do, in any convenient receptacle. The chair then inquires if all have voted who wish to, so as to be sure that the tellers have not missed any members. When all have voted that wish, he announces that "the polls are closed," and the tellers count the ballots, and the first one appointed reports the vote, as described on page 196, under Voting by Ballot. The chair then announces as elected all the candidates who received a majority vote, and the temporary officers are immediately replaced by the permanent ones elected. If the president is elected on this first ballot he immediately takes the chair. In case any of the offices remain unfilled, the chair immediately orders the tellers to distribute blank ballots, and directs the assembly to prepare ballots for these offices. Balloting is continued until all the offices are filled. The voting is not limited to the nominees, as every member is at liberty to vote for any member who is not declared ineligible by the by-laws.

After the offices are filled, if there is business that the chair knows requires immediate attention, he should mention it. Committees should probably be appointed for various purposes, as described in the by-laws, and the place of meeting should be determined. It is possible that an adjourned meeting may be necessary in order to complete the organization before beginning the regular work of the society. When the work is completed, or when an adjourned meeting has been provided for, and the lateness of the hour requires an adjournment, some one should move to adjourn. If the motion is carried, the chair announces the vote and declares the assembly adjourned. If there can be any question as to where and when the next meeting is to be held, he should mention the place and time, though this is not necessary afterwards when the place and time are regularly established and known.

If the society is one that expects to own real estate, it should be incorporated according to the laws of the state in which it is situated, and for this purpose some member of the committee on the constitution should consult a lawyer before this second meeting, so that the constitution may conform to the laws of the state. In this case the trustees, or managers, or directors, are usually instructed to take the proper measures to have the society incorporated.

(*c*) *Regular Meetings of a Society.* After a society is properly organized, its regular business meetings are conducted as follows: When the hour fixed for the meeting to begin arrives, the presiding officer takes the chair and calls the meeting to order and directs the secretary to read the minutes of the last meeting. When they are read, he asks, "Are there any corrections to the minutes?" If none are suggested, he adds, "There being none, the minutes stand approved as read." If any corrections are suggested, the secretary makes them, unless there is opposition. If there is difference of opinion, some one moves to amend the minutes, or the chair, without waiting for a motion, may put the question on the amendment that has been suggested. When this has been settled, the chair asks, "Are there any further corrections (or amendments) to the minutes?" If there is no response, he adds, "There being none, the minutes stand approved as corrected." He then announces the next business in order, following the order of business prescribed by the rules of the society.

If the order of business is the same as given in **65**, as soon as the minutes are read and approved, the chair says, "The next business in order is hearing the reports of the standing committees." He may then call upon each committee in its order for a report, thus: "Has the committee on applications for membership any report to make?" In this case the committee may report as shown above, or some member of it reply that it has no report to make. Or, when the chairman knows that there are but few, if any, reports to be made, it is better, after making the announcement of the business, for him to ask, "Have these committees any reports to make?" After a short pause, if no one rises to report, he states, "There being no reports from the standing committees, the next business in order is hearing the reports of special committees," when he will act the same as in the case of the standing committees. The chairman should always have a list of the committees, to enable him to call upon them, as well as to guide him in the appointment of new committees.

Having attended to the reports of committees, the chair announces the next business in order, and so on until the business of the meeting has been disposed of, when some one moves to adjourn. If this motion is carried, the chair announces the vote and declares the assembly adjourned.

The meetings of different societies vary greatly, and they should be managed differently in order to obtain the best results. Some societies require a strict enforcement of parliamentary rules, while with others the best results will be obtained by being informal. It is important that the presiding officer have tact and common sense, especially with a very intelligent assembly.

71. Meeting of a Convention or Assembly of Delegates. (*a*) *An Organized Convention.* If a convention is an organized body (that is, if when convened it has a constitution and by-laws and officers), a committee on credentials, or registration, and one on program, should have been appointed previous to the meeting. These committees may have been appointed at the previous convention, or by the executive board, or by the president, as prescribed by the by-laws. The committee on credentials, or registration, should be on hand somewhat before the time of the meeting, in some cases the day before, so as to be prepared to submit its report immediately after the opening addresses. It should furnish each delegate, when he registers, with a badge or card as evidence of his being a delegate and having the right of admission to the hall. The committee on program should in most cases have the programs printed in advance. In many cases it is better that the constituent bodies be furnished in advance with copies of the program. This should always be done when there is difficulty in getting full delegations to attend. In addition to these two committees there are a number of local committees usually appointed by the local society, as on entertainment, etc. One of the general officers usually performs the duty of a committee on transportation, to obtain reductions in railroad fares, etc.

When the hour appointed for the meeting arrives, the president, as the permanent presiding officer of a convention is usually called, stands at the desk, and, striking it with the gavel to attract attention, says, "The convention will come to order." In large conventions there is usually much confusion and noise at the opening, and it requires self-control, firmness, and tact on the part of the presiding officer to preserve proper order so that all members may hear and be heard. It is a mistake for the chairman to try to stop the noise by pounding with the gavel and talking so loud as to be heard in spite of conversation on the floor. It is better for him to set the example of being quiet, and to stop all business while the noise is such that members cannot hear. Members should be required to be seated and to refrain from talking except when addressing the chair.

When the convention has come to order it is customary to have some opening exercises, the nature of which depends upon the character of the convention. In the majority of cases the convention is opened with prayer, an address of welcome, and a response. The program, however, is the president's guide as to the order of business, even though it has not yet been adopted by the convention. It should provide for hearing the report of the credential committee as soon as the opening exercises are concluded, so that it may be known who are entitled to vote. This committee's report usually consists merely of a list of the delegates and their alternates, if any, whose credentials have been found correct, and of the ex-officio members of the convention, no one being on the list, however, who has not registered as present. The constitution should always provide that such as are present of the officers of the convention, the members of the Board of Managers, and the chairmen of the committees that are required to report at the convention, shall be ex-officio members of the convention.

When this report of the credential committee is presented it is read either by the chairman of the committee or by the reading secretary, or official reader, if there is one. In all cases, it, and all other reports, should be read from the platform. When the chairman of a committee cannot read so as to be heard, the report should be read by a reading secretary, or official reader, who should be appointed in every large convention, solely for the purpose of reading resolutions, reports, etc. If there is a case of contest between two sets of delegates and there is serious doubt as to which is entitled to recognition, the committee should omit both from the list and report the fact of the contest. If the committee, however, thinks the contest not justified, it should ignore it and enter on the list the names of the legitimate delegates. A motion should be made to accept or adopt the report, which, after it is stated by the chair, is open to debate and amendment. No one can vote whose name is not on the list of delegates reported by the committee. Upon the motion to substitute one delegation for another, neither one can vote. So upon a motion to strike out the names of a delegation whose seats are contested they cannot vote. But upon the main motion to accept the report, all persons whose names are on the list of members as reported by the committee and amended by the convention are entitled to vote, and they alone. When this report has been adopted, the president should immediately call upon the program committee for a report. The chairman of that committee submits the printed program and moves, or some one else moves, its adoption. This is open to debate and amendment, and when once adopted by a majority vote can not be deviated from except by a two-thirds vote of those voting, or by a majority vote of the enrolled membership.

The membership of the convention and the program having been decided, the convention is ready for its business as laid down in the program. The two committees, though they have made their reports, are continued through the session, as supplementary reports may be required from them. Additional delegates may arrive, and speakers on the program may be sick or unable to be present, or for other reasons a change in the program may be necessary. These two committees should be allowed at any time to make additional reports. The business is conducted as described in the preceding section, but, of course, the program must be followed. Boards and standing committees and the treasurer are always required to submit annual reports, and sometimes reports are required from various other officers. Generally officers and the board of managers, etc., are elected annually; but some constitutions make the term of office two years, and some provide, in addition, that only about half the officers shall be elected at any one annual meeting. In most organizations it is better to have the term of office begin at the close of the convention, so that the same officers will serve throughout the meetings. At the beginning of the first meeting each day the minutes of the preceding day are read and approved. At the close of the convention, if there is not time to read the minutes of the last day, a motion should be adopted authorizing the board, or some committee, to approve the minutes of that day. As the proceedings of a convention are usually published, a publishing committee should be appointed, which should have the power to edit the proceedings. When through with its business the convention adjourns sine die.

(*b*) *A Convention not yet Organized.* Such a convention is similar to a mass meeting, already described in **69**, in that when called to order it has no constitution, by-laws, or officers. It has the added difficulty of determining who are entitled to vote. In the mass meeting every one may vote, but in the convention none but properly appointed delegates may vote, and sometimes this is a very difficult question to determine justly.

The convention must have been called by some committee, or body of men, who should have secured the hall and made the preliminary arrangements for the meeting. If the convention is a very large one, so that it is necessary to reserve the main floor of the hall for the delegates, the committee should allow only those to enter who have prima facie evidence of their right to membership, and in contested cases both sides should be admitted. The chairman of the committee should call the convention to order, and either he or some one the committee has selected for the purpose should nominate a temporary chairman and a temporary secretary. Next should come the appointment of a committee on credentials, whose duty it is to examine all credentials and report a list of all the delegates who are entitled to seats in the convention. When alternates have been appointed they should be reported also. While the committee on credentials is out, committees may be appointed on nominations of officers, on rules, and on order of business or program. In a large convention of this kind all committees should be appointed by the chair, and no one whose right to a seat is questioned should be placed on a committee until the convention has acted favorably on his case. Until the committee on credentials has reported, no business can be done except to authorize the chair to appoint the above mentioned committees. While waiting for the committee on credentials to report, the time is usually spent in listening to speeches. When the committee reports, the procedure is the same as just described in an organized convention. When that report has been adopted, the convention proceeds to its permanent organization, acting upon the reports of the other three committees previously appointed, taking them in such order as the convention pleases. When these reports have been acted upon, the convention is organized, with members, officers, rules, and program, and its business is transacted as in other organized deliberative assemblies. If the convention adopts rules only for the session, the committee on rules need recommend only a few rules as to the hours for beginning the meetings, the length of the speeches, etc., and a rule adopting some standard rules of order, where not in conflict with its other rules. If it is not intended to make a permanent organization, the organization just described is all that is necessary.

If the convention is called to make a permanent organization, the committee on nominations is not appointed until after the by-laws are adopted, and the committee on rules should report a constitution and by-laws as in the case of a permanent society [70]. The committee in such case is more usually called the committee on constitution and by-laws. When a convention of this kind is composed of delegates away from their homes it is practically impossible to have them assemble more frequently than once a year, and, therefore, before the convention meets, a constitution and by-laws should be carefully drafted by those interested in calling the convention. Those who drew up the by-laws should be appointed on the committee, in order to avoid delay in reporting them.

After the committee has reported a constitution and by-laws the procedure is the same as already described in the previous section in case of acting on a constitution and by-laws for a permanent society [page 287]. When the by-laws are adopted, the officers are elected and committees are appointed as prescribed by the by-laws, and the convention is prepared for its work as already described.

Art. XIII. Legal Rights of Assemblies and Trial of Their Members.

72. The Right of a Deliberative Assembly to Punish its Members. A deliberative assembly has the inherent right to make and enforce its own laws and punish an offender, the extreme penalty, however, being expulsion from its own body. When expelled, if the assembly is a permanent society, it has the right, for its own protection, to give public notice that the person has ceased to be a member of that society.

But it has no right to go beyond what is necessary for self-protection and publish the charges against the member. In a case where a member of a society was expelled, and an officer of the society published, by its order, a statement of the grave charges upon which he had been found guilty, the expelled member recovered damages from the officer in a suit for libel, the court holding that the truth of the charges did not affect the case.

73. Right of an Assembly to Eject any one from its Place of Meeting. Every deliberative assembly has the right to decide who may be present during its session; and when the assembly, either by a rule or by a vote, decides that a certain person shall not remain in the room, it is the duty of the chairman to enforce the rule of order, using whatever force is necessary to eject the party.

The chairman can detail members to remove the person, without calling upon the police. If, however, in enforcing the order, any one uses harsher measures than is necessary to remove the person, the courts have held that he, and he alone, is liable for damages, just the same as a policeman would be under similar circumstances. However badly the man may be abused while being removed from the room, neither the chairman nor the society is liable for damages, as, in ordering his removal, they did not exceed their legal rights.

74. **Rights of Ecclesiastical Tribunals.** Many of our deliberative assemblies are ecclesiastical bodies, and it is important to know how much respect will be paid to their decisions by the civil courts.

A church became divided, and each party claimed to be the church, and therefore entitled to the church property. The case was taken into the civil courts, and finally, on appeal, to the U. S. Supreme Court, which, after holding the case under advisement for a year, sustained the decision of the U. S. Circuit Court. The Supreme Court, in rendering its decision, laid down the broad principle that when a local church is but a part of a large and more general organization or denomination, the court will accept as final the decision of the highest ecclesiastical tribunal to which the case has been carried within that general church organization, on all questions of discipline, faith, or ecclesiastical rule, custom, or law, and will not inquire into the justice or injustice of its decree as between the parties before it. The officers, the ministers, the members, or the church body which the highest judiciary of the denomination recognizes, the court will recognize. Whom that body expels or cuts off, the court will hold to be no longer members of that church. The court laid down the following principles: *

---

* Watson vs. Jones, 13 Wallace U. S. Supreme Court Reports, p. 679. This case was decided April 15, 1872.

"Where a church is of a strictly congregational or independent organization, and the property held by it has no trust attached to it, its right to the use of the property must be determined by the ordinary principles which govern ordinary associations.

"Where the local congregation is itself a member of a much larger and more important religious organization and is under its government and control and is bound by its orders and judgments, its decisions are final and binding on legal tribunals.

"Courts having no ecclesiastical jurisdiction, cannot revise or question ordinary acts of church discipline; their only judicial power arises from the conflicting claims of the parties to the church property and the use of it."

But while the civil courts have no ecclesiastical jurisdiction, and cannot revise or question ordinary acts of church discipline, they do have jurisdiction where there are conflicting claims to church property. An independent church by an almost unanimous vote decided to unite with another independent church. A very small minority, less than ten per cent, did not wish to unite with the other church, so they were voted letters of dismission to any other church of like faith and order, against their protest. The majority then directed the trustees to transfer their property to the other church and voted themselves a letter of dismission to unite with that church. The church then voted to disband. The majority presented their letters and were received into the other church. The minority would not use their letters, but took the matter into the courts, which, of course, decided that they were the church and owned the property. According to the practice of churches of the same denomination, no member can be forced out of the church unless for neglect of his duties as a member. Letters of dismission are granted only on the request of members, and as a general rule the membership does not terminate until the letter has been used. The church could not terminate the membership of the minority, against whom there were no charges, by voting them letters without their consent. By not using their letters they soon constituted the entire membership and rescinded the order to the trustees to transfer the property to the other church. By the hasty, ill-advised action of almost the entire church the majority lost their property. In cases where property is involved, churches cannot be too careful, and it is usually best to act under legal advice.

75. Trial of Members of Societies. Every deliberative assembly, having the right to purify its own body, must therefore have the right to investigate the character of its members. It can require any of them to testify in the case, under pain of expulsion if they refuse.

When the charge is against the member's character, it is usually referred to a committee of investigation or discipline, or to some standing committee, to report upon. Some societies have standing committees whose duty it is to report cases for discipline whenever any are known to them.

In either case, the committee investigates the matter and reports to the society. This report need not go into details, but should contain its recommendations as to what action the society should take, and should usually close with resolutions covering the case, so that there is no need for any one to offer any additional resolutions upon it. The ordinary resolutions, where the member is recommended to be expelled, are (1) to fix the time to which the society shall adjourn;

and (2) to instruct the clerk to cite the member to appear before the society at this adjourned meeting to show cause why he should not be expelled, upon the following charges which should then be given.

After charges are preferred against a member, and the assembly has ordered that he be cited to appear for trial, he is theoretically under arrest, and is deprived of all the rights of membership until his case is disposed of. Without his consent no member should be tried at the same meeting at which the charges are preferred, excepting when the charges relate to something done at that meeting.

The clerk should send the accused a written notice to appear before the society at the time appointed, and should at the same time furnish him with a copy of the charges. A failure to obey the summons is generally cause enough for summary expulsion.

At the appointed meeting what may be called the trial takes place. Frequently the only evidence required against the member is the report of the committee. After it has been read and any additional evidence offered that the committee may see fit to introduce, the accused should be allowed to make an explanation and introduce witnesses, if he so desires. Either party should be allowed to cross-examine the other's witnesses and introduce rebutting testimony. When the evidence is all in, the accused should retire from the room, and the society deliberate upon the question, and finally act by a vote upon the question of expulsion, or other punishment proposed. No member should be expelled by less than a two-thirds* vote, a quorum voting. The vote should be by ballot, except

* The U. S. Constitution [Art. I, Sec. 5] provides that each House of Congress may, "with the concurrence of two-thirds, expel a member."

by general consent. The members of the committee preferring the charges vote the same as other members.

In acting upon the case, it must be borne in mind that there is a vast distinction between the evidence necessary to convict in a civil court and that required to convict in an ordinary society or ecclesiastical body. A notorious pickpocket could not even be arrested, much less convicted by a civil court, simply on the ground of being commonly known as a pickpocket; while such evidence would convict and expel him from any ordinary society.

The moral conviction of the truth of the charge is all that is necessary in an ecclesiastical or other deliberative body to find the accused guilty of the charges.

If the trial is liable to be long and troublesome, or of a very delicate nature, the member is frequently cited to appear before a committee, instead of the society, for trial. In this case the committee reports to the society the result of its trial of the case, with resolutions covering the punishment which it recommends the society to adopt. When the committee's report is read, the accused should be permitted to make his statement of the case, the committee being allowed to reply. The accused then retires from the room, and the society acts upon the resolutions submitted by the committee. The members of the committee should vote upon the case the same as other members.

If the accused wishes counsel at his trial, it is usual to allow it, provided the counsel is a member of the society in good standing. Should the counsel be guilty of improper conduct during the trial, the society can refuse to hear him, and can also punish him.

PLAN FOR STUDY OF PARLIAMENTARY LAW

INTRODUCTION.

These Lesson Outlines are designed to assist clubs and individual students who wish to study Robert's Rules of Order Revised. The Manual is not arranged primarily with a view to study, but for the special object of providing a set of rules for adoption by city councils, corporations, literary societies, clubs, assemblies, and occasional meetings. In studying it the preferable way is to learn the few elementary things that one must know in order to take the slightest part in a deliberative meeting and then to learn how with ease to use this Manual to find the correct ruling or decision on any point that may arise. When one has accomplished this, which is covered by the first four lessons outlined below, he is prepared to study in detail any portion of the Manual, and in any order that may suit him.

In these Lesson Outlines the four introductory lessons are followed by the all-important subject of Amendments, to which an entire lesson is given. This lesson should be thoroughly mastered, as the subject of amendments is probably equal in difficulty and importance to all the rest of parliamentary law.

After Amendments, the order of the subjects in the Manual is followed in the Lesson Outlines with the following exceptions: Incidental Motions are not taken up until all the other motions are disposed of; the Orders of the Day are treated in connection with the motions to Postpone Definitely and Indefinitely, because they are so intimately connected, the Orders of the Day being made by postponing to a certain time or by adopting a program; the subject of Committees is treated in connection with the motion to Commit; and to Take from the Table is treated in connection with to Lay on the Table.

The Rules of Order is essentially a work of

reference, and the student should keep this in view. He should aim at learning how to find a ruling quickly, rather than at remembering the ruling. On this account each student should always have his copy of the book with him at every meeting and familiarize himself with its use. Efficiency, however, as a parliamentarian is acquired only by practice. "Book knowledge" is valuable just as with games and athletics, but just as no amount of theoretical knowledge without practice will enable a man to excel in playing chess or in swimming, so no amount of theoretical knowledge of parliamentary law without practice will make a man a good practical parliamentarian.

If the student has the advantage of being a member of a class, the teacher will, doubtless, use parliamentary drills. If he has no teacher, he should study the Manual as laid down in the Lesson Outlines, and try to interest others to join him in forming a practice club. This practice club should hold frequent meetings, thus giving an opportunity for putting into practice what has been learned. The officers should be constantly changed so as to give different members the opportunity to preside.

These practice meetings should begin at least as soon as the students have learned what is covered by the first four lessons as outlined further on. At the beginning of each meeting it would be profitable to call for criticisms of the previous meeting. This would encourage the members after each meeting to investigate all doubtful points that have arisen, and would call attention to mistakes that otherwise would be overlooked.

What has just been said in reference to the importance of practice meetings or drills in parliamentary law applies equally to clubs or societies, as only a few of the simplest rules are usually called for in an ordinary meeting. When the club cannot have a suitable teacher, it can carry on the work by electing a member to take charge of the parliamentary drills. This leader should study the course so as to be able to take the place of a teacher.

It will probably be best in all cases to follow the order of the first four lessons, and perhaps the fifth also. But where the time for the meeting is short, it may be advisable to increase the number of lessons. After the fifth lesson circumstances may make it advisable to select only a few out of the remaining lessons and omit the others, or to divide some of the lessons. The outlines as given will serve as a basis for a scheme of lessons adapted to the special conditions in each case.

All through the course there should constantly be drills with open books, to enable the students to acquire facility in referring to a desired point, since, as previously stated, this Manual is a work of reference.

LESSON OUTLINES

I

Organizing and Conducting Business in Mass Meetings and Permanent Societies.

Organization, pp. 275-277.
Offering, Amending, and Adopting Resolutions, pp. 277-280.
Committee on Resolutions, pp. 280-283.
Permanent Society, 1st Meeting, pp. 284-286.
Permanent Society, 2d Meeting, pp. 286-291.
Permanent Society, Regular Meeting, pp. 291, 292.
Obtaining the Floor, etc., pp. 25-28.
Preparing, Making, and Seconding Motions and Resolutions, pp. 33-38.

II.

Debate, Stating and Putting Questions, and What Motions to Use to Accomplish Certain Objects.

Stating the Question, p. 38.
Debate, pp. 38, 39.
Secondary Motions, p. 40.
Putting the Question and Announcing the Vote, pp. 40-43.
What Motions to Use to Accomplish Certain Objects, pp. 43-51.

[The form of making each of these motions should be explained by the leader or teacher.]

III.

How to Find if a Motion is in Order, if it can be Debated, Amended, or Reconsidered, and if it Requires a Second, or a ⅔ Vote, etc.

Order of Precedence of Motions, p. 5.
Table of Rules Relating to Motions, pp. 6-12.

[The order of Precedence of Motions, p. 5, should be memorized, and the student should be able by reference to the Table of Rules to find quickly the ruling on any of the 300 questions decided by it.]

IV.

Definitions, and How to Find Rulings in the Manual.

Plan of the Manual, pp. 20-22.
Definitions, pp. 22-24.
Plan of the Index, p. 313.
Practice in the Use of the Entire Manual for finding Rulings or Decisions.

V.

Amendments.

Amend, pp. 134-152.
Inserting or adding, striking out, and striking out and inserting words, pp. 137-140.
Amendments affecting an entire paragraph, pp. 140-143.
Improper Amendments, pp. 143-146.
Motions that cannot be Amended, pp. 146, 147.
Amending Minutes, p. 148.
Filling Blanks, pp. 148-152.

VI.

Classification of Motions and Most of the Privileged Ones.

Main Motions, pp. 51-54.
Subsidiary Motions, pp. 54-56.
Incidental Motions, pp. 56, 57.
Privileged Motions, pp. 57, 58.
Certain Other Motions, p. 58.
Fix the Time to which to Adjourn, pp. 59, 60.
Adjourn, pp. 60-64.
Take a Recess, pp. 64-66.
Questions of Privilege, pp. 66-68.

VII.

Orders of the Day, and Definite and Indefinite Postponement.

Postpone Indefinitely, pp. 152, 153.
Postpone Definitely or to a Certain Time, pp. 121-125.
Call for the Orders of the Day, pp. 68-71.
General and Special Orders, pp. 71-77.

VIII.

Laying Aside a Question Temporarily, Resuming its Consideration, and Closing and Limiting Debate.

Lay on the Table, pp. 104-111.
Take from the Table, pp. 154-156.
Previous Question, pp. 111-118.
Limit or Extend Limits of Debate, pp. 118-120.

IX.

The Motion to Commit, and Committees.

Commit, pp. 125-134.
Special and Standing Committees, pp. 211-220.
Form of their Reports, pp. 215, 216.
Form of Minority Report, p. 216.

X.

Committees (Concluded).

Reception of Committees' Reports, pp. 220-223.
Adoption of Committees' Reports, pp. 223-229.
Committee of the Whole, pp. 229-233.
As if in Committee of the Whole, pp. 233, 234.
Informal Consideration, pp. 234, 235.
Committees Classified, pp. 206, 207.
Boards of Managers, etc., and Executive Committees, pp. 207-210.
Ex-Officio Members of Boards and Committees, p. 210.

XI.

Reconsidering and Rescinding a Vote.

Reconsider, pp. 156-165.
Reconsider and Enter on the Minutes, pp. 165-168.
Rescind, pp. 169, 170.

XII.

Some Miscellaneous and Incidental Motions.

Renew, pp. 171-173.
Ratify, pp. 173, 174.
Dilatory and Absurd Motions, pp. 174, 175.
Incidental Motions, pp. 56, 57.
Questions of Order, pp. 78-81.
Appeal, pp. 81-83.
Suspension of the Rules, pp. 83-87.

XIII.

Incidental Motions (Concluded).

Objection to the Consideration of a Question, pp. 87-89.
Division of a Question, pp. 89-92.
Consideration by Paragraph or Seriatim, pp. 92-95.
Division of the Assembly and Other Motions relating to Voting and the Polls, pp. 95, 96.
Motions relating to Methods of Making and to Closing and to Reopening Nominations, pp. 96, 97.
Parliamentary Inquiry, pp. 98, 99.
Request for Information, pp. 99, 100.
To Withdraw or Modify a Motion, pp. 100, 101.
To Read Papers, pp. 101, 102.
To be Excused from a Duty, pp. 102-104.
Request for any other Privilege, p. 104.

XIV.

Debate.

Debate, pp. 39 and 178-180.
Decorum in Debate, pp. 180-182.
Closing and Preventing Debate, pp. 182-184.
Principles of Debate, pp. 184-187.
Motions that Open the Main Question to Debate, p. 187.
Undebatable Motions, p. 187.

XV.

Voting.

Voting, pp. 188-201.
Announcing the Vote, pp. 190, 191.
Voting by Ballot, pp. 193-196.
Voting by Yeas and Nays, pp. 197, 198.
General Consent, pp. 198, 199.
Voting by Mail, pp. 199, 200.
Voting by Proxy, pp. 200, 201.
Votes that are Null and Void even if Unanimous, pp. 201, 202.
Motions requiring More than a Majority Vote, pp. 202-206.

XVI.

The Officers and the Minutes.

Chairman or President, pp. 236-244.
Hints to Inexperienced Chairmen, pp. **242-244.**
Secretary or Clerk, pp. 244-247.
Corresponding Secretary, p. 246.
The Minutes, pp. 247-250.
Executive Secretary, pp. 250, 251.
Treasurer, pp. 251-253.

XVII.

Nominations and Elections, and Miscellaneous.

Session, pp. 253-257.
Meeting, pp. 253-255.
Quorum, pp. 257-261.
Order of Business, pp. 261-263.
Nominations and Elections, pp. 263, 264.

[As the officers are usually elected by ballot that method of voting (pages 193-196) should be reviewed in connection with this lesson. The incidental motions relating to the methods of making nominations and taking the vote and of closing and reopening nominations and the polls (pages 95-97) should also be reviewed in connection with this lesson.]

XVIII.

Rules of an Assembly and their Amendments.

Constitutions, pp. 264-266.
By-laws, pp. 266, 267.
Rules of Order, pp. 267, 268.
Standing Rules and their Amendment, pp. 268, 269.
Amendment of Constitutions, etc., pp. 269-273.
Amending a Proposed Amendment to the Constitution, etc., p. 272.
Review Use of Tables on pages 5-10, and Index.

INDEX

—o—

The figures refer usually to the page where the treatment of the subject begins. The arrangement of the work can be most easily seen by examining the Table of Contents (pp. 1-4); its plan is explained in the Introduction (p. 20). If it is desired to find the proper motion to use to accomplish a certain object, turn to page 44. On pages 5-10 will be found a large amount of information about all the motions in common use, which should be carefully studied so that when the facts are needed they can be quickly found. On those pages will be found, among other things, the circumstances under which any of the common motions may be made; the motions that are in order while a specified motion is pending; and whether a specified motion may be debated, amended, or reconsidered, and whether it requires a two-thirds vote, etc. In the Index under the title, "Motions, List of," will be found a complete list of motions. To find the details refer to the particular motion in the Index. It is best always to refer to general subjects first, as under them will usually be found all the details. Look under Adjourn, Committee, Debate, Forms, Vote, etc., for illustrations.

———o———